In Region Training: Travels in Sub-Saharan Africa

Arnold Hammari

DEDICATION

This book is dedicated to my lovely wife Megan who has supported me during the many years I have spent alone in Africa while taking care of the house, kids, pets and everything else.

CONTENTS

ACKNOWLEDGMENTS

I would like to acknowledge the hard work of my editor, Richard Sonnenfeld, who spent hours reviewing, editing, and making suggestions for this manuscript. I must also thank my mentor and frequent travel companion, Brad Nicholson, for encouraging me to rework my journal and share it with the world.

i

INTRODUCTION

This book is a copy of my journal during my travels in Africa from July 2010 to July 2011 while I worked at the U.S. Embassy in Dakar, Senegal. My mission for that year was to travel and learn as much as possible about Africa in order to become an African expert. I had a budget of $40,000 and a cohort of colleagues stationed in different locations around the African continent with similar missions. We often traveled together to reduce expenses and the impact to our hosts.

I tried to balance my trips between meeting with local officials, visiting U.S. activities in the local area, and experiencing the cultural highlights of the country. I paid for all of the fun adventures out of my pocket and did not use government funds for non-official activities. Due to work confidentiality issues I can't detail in this book all of my meetings and official business but I can share the more interesting experiences with the reader.

During the course of one year I visited 20 countries in Africa transiting by train, plane, automobile, speedboat, and on foot. I climbed Kilimanjaro, ran the Accra marathon, surfed Cameroon, dove shipwrecks, met gorillas in the mist, and snorkeled with whale sharks. I also met many interesting people, learned about their cultures and traditions, and studied regional security issues.

Before I would visit each country I would read three to four books about the country and related issues and ask questions of the people I met on my travels. I took copious notes, which were very valuable in my graduate degree in International Relations and African Studies at Boston University. One year later I had the amazing opportunity to visit Uganda to conduct research before writing my master's thesis on Counterinsurgency and the Lord's Resistance Army, tying in many of my experiences in Africa.

Since completing my studies I have worked in the U.S. Embassy in N'Djamena, Chad and at United States Africa Command where in my current job I continue to visit various countries on the African continent and work Africa-related security issues. Traveling in Africa has formed my thoughts and baseline of my work on the continent.

-Camp Lemonnier, Djibouti
7 December 2015

1 WELCOME TO AFRICA

Dakar, Senegal. 5-9 July 2010.

We celebrated Independence Day with family and friends but it was also a farewell party for me. Early the next morning I boarded a plane from New Hampshire through Washington DC for Dakar, Senegal on the African continent. I arranged for 1000 lbs. of food, gear, and clothes to be shipped by airfreight to Dakar and I carried the rest with me on the plane: three surfboards, my laptop computer, and a weeks' worth of clothes in a duffle bag.

I had been selected for a special internship at the US Embassy in Dakar with a mission to explore Africa over the course of a year. Dakar would serve as my home base, I had a budget of $40,000 and a Toyota Landcruiser to see as much as I could. When I was in Dakar I was expected to help out at the Embassy, but my main mission was to learn about Africa through travel and meeting local Africans. In order to qualify for this internship I had just completed an Associate's Degree in French and could also fall back on my Portuguese language experiences from living in Brazil for a couple years. The three main colonial languages in Africa were French, English, and Portuguese and I could speak all three fluently, but unfortunately the colonial languages were often a second or third language for the locals. In Dakar the locals spoke Wolof amongst themselves and French as a second language. English was not commonly spoken in Senegal and at times I had to act as a translator and tour guide for visiting VIPs from the US.

I arrived in Dakar after midnight on a South African Airlines flight that prepared us for the heat of Africa by turning off the air conditioning in the middle of the flight. So when they cracked the door in Senegal to let us off the plane there wasn't a change in temperature but a wave of humidity that flooded in to the back of the plane and immediately saturated your clothing. Leopold Senghor Airport is located in the upscale Almadies neighborhood seven miles from downtown Dakar and next to the massive African Renaissance statue of a ripped African man holding his wife and child pointing to the west. Dim yellow lights illuminated the base of the statue and the terminal but the rest of the flight line and neighborhood was pitch black and very quiet.

Thankfully my contact at the U.S. Embassy had arranged for an expediter to meet me at customs and walked my passport through immigration and the three hundred other passengers on my flight. In the baggage claim area we were swarmed by porters who wanted to carry our bags but only spoke enough English to say "come with me." The expediter yelled at them in Wolof and they left me alone. Once I stepped outside the terminal I was met by a wall of taxi drivers shouting to be heard over each other and reaching out to grab you or waving their hands to get your attention. There was a metal barricade separating them from the entry way but it felt like going through a gauntlet with people yelling at you in a variety of languages. My contact, Delvin, met me outside the fray in a Toyota Landcruiser and quickly sped me off through the dark streets to his apartment near the beach.

Five hours later, I put on slacks and button-up shirt, and Delvin drove me to the Embassy to meet the different offices and check on my living arrangements. Rush hour traffic in Dakar was a shock as we drove along the coast from Almadies to the embassy. There were no traffic signals and a few traffic circles allowed traffic to branch off the crowded four-lane road. Nobody signaled and a variety of broken down rusty taxis billowing huge clouds of black and gray smoke caused blockages when they stopped to take on or let off passengers. Expatriates and the few rich elite Senegalese attempted to carve their way through traffic in their expensive SUVs and European luxury cars but still got stuck in the traffic jam as well. The traffic that morning was especially bad as the part of the road by the fishing village was blocked by fishermen demonstrating against the fatal shooting of a fisherman by the coast guard for fishing in a restricted area. Demonstrators blocked the road by setting tires on fire and throwing rocks at passing cars and were eventually dispersed by riot police with teargas, batons, and water cannons on armored vehicles.

The embassy is located in the downtown neighborhood known as "Plateau" next to the national assembly building, presidential palace, and the Catholic cathedral. I got a special visa for my year in Senegal put in my passport and was assigned an apartment in a building that overlooks the presidential palace. When I went to check out the building I discovered a dozen armed guards and Senegalese Police in the lobby as the President's son owned the penthouse apartment and he had some of his offices in the same building. I was given the keys to the two-bedroom apartment on the third floor of the building and had balconies that overlooked the downtown mosque on one side and a nightclub on the other. Since my apartment was empty and furniture wouldn't be delivered until later in the week we headed back to Delvin's apartment in Almadies. He handed me the keys to the Landcruiser, said "good luck," and left me on my own to negotiate the streets of Dakar.

I found my way back to Delvin's apartment, again at rush hour, with a detour past the port, industrial zone, soccer stadium, and the airport without getting into an accident. At the airport the road was blocked for a couple minutes as a boy drove a herd of cattle down the road to bring them home from the pasture. The nice thing about driving a big SUV is that the little cars and scooters get out of your way, even if they have the right of way. Another thing is that the plush Landcruiser suspension soaked up the bumps from the cratered roads and many speed bumps.

Since Delvin's house was practically on the beach I decided to go for a walk to check out the local surf breaks. Dakar became famous for its waves in the 1966 surf movie "Endless Summer" that features a pair of California surfers who try to follow the summer and waves around the world. The first place they land in Africa is Dakar and they surf the waves off N'Gor Island in Almadies. N'Gor Island was about a mile north of Delvin's apartment so I decided to see if I could find a good break for surfing and found a decent break about a 1/4-mile up the road. The waves were about knee high and there was a body boarder and a knee boarder taking turns catching a fast short wave. The rides weren't that long but it was doable. I talked to a guy that worked at a bar in front of the break and he said there was a swell coming in and the break worked best at high tide (around 10 am tomorrow).

I walked down the beach another 1/4 mile and just over a small hill from the last break was a larger sandy beach with about waist high sets breaking about 50 meters from some rocks. It looked like with a different tide and larger sets it could be a long, fast hollow wave. Nobody was on it, so maybe there was some other hidden danger I couldn't see.

As I approached the beach a local guy was walking past me and stopped me by asking what I thought of the waves. Since surfing is my favorite topic and it gave me a chance to practice my French I decided to see what he had to say. He agreed with the previous prediction of a coming swell and said he could show me a better break up the road. As we walked I asked him questions about surfing since he said he surfed too but he had no ideas about the famous breaks by N'Gor. Since his English was pretty good (he was correcting my French in English) I asked him what he did for a living. When he responded that he was a tour guide I knew that he was going to try to scam me. But I decided to play along just to see what it was like to be scammed and because he was easy to talk to and I could practice my French. Back in the states people were paying $80 an hour for a French tutor, so this would be a bargain!

We walked up the next rise along the beach and even though it provided a better viewpoint of the coast, the waves weren't any better. After talking about the monument and the other cool things you could see from that overlook point, about 30 minutes after I met the guy he pulled a necklace out of his pocket and tells me he wants to give me a present. I should have walked away again at that point, but I wanted to see how this would play out.

After he had put it around my neck despite my mild protests, I started to thank him for his time and tried to walk away but he stopped me. He said he was giving me this present because his wife just gave birth to his first son, named Mustafa, and he was going to have a big party for all his relatives and he wanted me to give him a gift. I decided to give him 1000 CFAs (about $2) and when I pulled the note out of my pocket he saw I had another bill in my pocket too. He took the 1000 CFA note and rubbed it on my forehead, then his own forehead, and declared it was a way to bless me or pray for me. He insisted it was his culture to bring good luck or blessings to rub money on my forehead and his. He then asked to see the other note so he could pray for it too. I told him no and walked away, but he ran right after me and became more and more insistent in his need to bless my money and said that I was offending him and his culture by not letting him see my money. After him following me for five minutes with him becoming more aggressive, and as we were out of sight from the road and others, I decided to give in and see if he would do what I thought he would. I handed him the 2000 CFA note (about $4) and he rubbed it on my forehead, then his own, and then put it in his pocket. Exactly what I thought he would do. I asked for my money back but he said he needed it to buy couscous for all his family coming to the party. As it was getting dark I walked away quickly back to the road and he finally left me alone. I knew what was going to happen based on what others had told me, but I wanted to try it out for myself and experience it firsthand. I figured I only had 3000 CFAs to risk and it was a good lesson in French as well as street scams.

I spent the next couple days exploring Dakar, finding boulangeries (bread and pastry vendor), a hardware store, and several fish and meet markets. The real surprise was walking into the air conditioned shopping center (Dakar center in Les Almadies) which has coffee shops, a nice store to buy a suit, a sports store with everything Nike, and a European style supermarket where you can buy your Salmon and French cheeses as well as 32" flat screen TVs. Prices for the local items weren't that bad for local items. For example local yogurt cost about $0.50 each but the imported yogurt was $1.25 each. Not much different from grocery prices in Hawaii. The salmon for 172,500 CFAs was too much though, but they had it!

Dakar, Senegal. 11 July 2010.

By the end of my first week in Senegal my loaner furniture and the food and few personal goods I had shipped from America arrived and I was able to move into my apartment. All my furniture was delivered before 9am and then the items I shipped airfreight arrived at 10am so I spent the morning unpacking and getting situated.

Around lunch I started to get hungry so I decided to go to the local supermarket to buy some bleach, bread, and vegetables- but I couldn't find the huge Casino supermarket downtown. After walking for 30 minutes and ignoring all the people who wanted me as their friend to buy something from them, a man named Ali asked if I was a guest at the hotel where he worked. It was a different approach and I figured if he thought I was a guest at the hotel he wouldn't try to take advantage of me. He mentioned his African garb was required as a worker at the hotel and I complimented him on his appearance as it was nice and he offered to help me find the market.

Instead of taking me to the Casino supermarket he took me to a huge outdoor market downtown. Ali, my guide, said it was one of the largest ones around and was more than a square kilometer in size. He asked what I wanted to buy and we set off in search of bleach. After visiting 4 or 5 stalls on the main road, we headed off into the darker and narrower allies, until we were walking behind the stalls and buildings. Even these little places didn't have bleach. I was getting worried as this was getting more precarious and Ali was talking mostly Wolof to the people in the shops so I couldn't understand what was going on.

Eventually Ali guided me back onto the main road of the market in front of a large textile factory, which according to Ali, belonged to his father. Ali led me into the building and it was packed with people, fabric, and sewing machines. On each floor of the five-floor building were rooms full of young men and their sewing machines. They sewed all kinds of local clothing and more western attire as well. They made bags, blankets, towels- everything you could think of. I don't think it was sweatshop, but in Africa it was hot and everyone was sweating (but keeping their work clean). In the middle of the tour one of the shopkeepers from the open-air market showed up with a bottle of bleach and said it cost 4000 CFAs (about $8 for a 1 little bottle). I countered by saying that I had seen it in the stores for 2000 CFAs, but Ali said he would settle it at 3000 CFAs- a compromise. I went along with it as the guy had to run to the nearby Casino supermarket and track us down to get it to me (that must have been their conversation in Wolof, Ali would steer me away to his shop and his buddy would run to the store and they would meet up at the factory- I must have SUCKER written all over me).

Ali then began his sales pitch to get me to buy several of his shirts at a great price he would negotiate for me. He wouldn't tell me how much the shirts cost until I found one that I liked and then he stated they cost 15,000 CFAs ($30) each, and I should buy several. We negotiated some and I stuck firm at 5000 CFAs, which he finally accepted. He kept pressuring me to get more, but I reassured him that I would be back since he had showed me his great factory and I would be living here for a year. He probably didn't believe I would be back because most of the people around here, I found out later in the day, get the same shirts for about 2000 CFAs each.

Later that afternoon I fought my way through traffic to Les Almadies to go surfing for the first time in Africa. I stopped and paddled out at the first break that had people on it and struggled to catch some waves. The problems were two-fold, it was a new spot for me and I didn't know the currents and rocks but also the spot was dominated by lightweight kids on body boards who managed to float above the coral to get on the wave. Eventually I shifted over to a spot right in front of the bar on the beach to where a couple surfers were catching some overhead waves. I quickly discovered that you had to take are hard right as soon as the wave broke because you were 50 feet from the rocks. And that was just the visible danger- I caught one wave and bailed I thought a safe distance from the rocks but was pushed into some rocks just under the surface and found some sea urchins who embedded a couple quills in my hand. I still surfed until dark.

The next day I finally made it to the Casino supermarket in Les Almadies and discovered that the one liter bottle of bleach that Ali the guide arranged for me for 3000 CFAs actually only cost 450 CFAs. It made me kind of bitter. Almost everyone I have talked to has only wanted to steal from me. Where to do I find the good locals? People I can trust?

I got a couple sacks of groceries for 5250 CFAs, including some fresh bread and pain de chocolate. I checked the tribal surf shop, but it was closed again- I have been there 3 times and it has never been open. I ended up at the "secret spot," one break north of the last place I surfed and it was full of kids as well, but more expats- probably because it was Saturday. Again the break was close to the shore, but I got a couple waist high waves. It was pretty chaotic, until one expat yelled at me for cutting in the lineup, when it had been a free-for-all all day long. People were paddling around and snaking each other, three or more going for the same wave. I followed his instructions and got the next wave, but it carried me into some shallows and I stepped on an urchin when I bailed- about 20 thick needles jammed straight into the bottom of my left foot, so my day was over. It was going to be my last wave anyways but what a sour way to go.

As I cut into my foot with my Swiss Army knife while I sat on the tailgate of my Landcruiser in the parking lot some little local kid wandered up. He grabbed the tweezers and tried to grab the needles as I pried them up with the knife blade, but we could hardly get anything below the surface out. Every now and then some other local would wander up and try to sell me something- one guy even had a box of little yellow birds, but after about 30 minutes I gave up on my foot. I changed and tried to leave but all of a sudden my little friend wanted something- maybe payment for jamming the needles deeper in my foot as I sawed on it with a pocketknife. I don't really know because he used some words I didn't recognize, so I just left. I wasn't in the mood for handouts as the pain was starting to build and the adrenaline was wearing off.

When I got back to the apartment I looked up some treatments for close encounters with sea urchins and ended up pissing on my foot then trying to cook it in hot water for an hour or so. The weekend was pure agony with a throbbing foot and nothing I did or took for the pain helped. Ice was the only thing that kept the swelling and pain down.

Monday couldn't come soon enough and as soon as the clinic opened I hobbled across town to see the doctor. Luckily I have access to a good clinic with English speaking doctors. I was also fortunate to be seen right away by a doctor who said she liked pulling out urchin spines. After 90 minutes with a sterilized needle and tweezers the Doc finally got them all out. She said in some cases multiple spines were in the same hole. Most were over a 1/2 cm long and had gone straight into my foot. She kept saying, "This is not a joke."

Dakar, Senegal. 15 July 2010.

It took me a couple days before I was able to walk around without an obvious limp and I was willing to try out another cultural event. I went over to a friend's house for a mini cultural experience: their housekeeper made Thieboudienne, a delicious traditional Senegalese dish featuring a big fish, rice, shrimp, smaller fish balls, lots of fresh veggies (eggplant, cabbage, carrots, mandioc, potatoes, etc...), and incorporated in a tomato and peanut sauce. The fish is called "Capitaine," also known as Nile Perch, and tasted great, as did the whole meal. It was my first experience with Capitaine and the fish wasn't flaky and did not have a fishy flavor. It took her 6 hours to make it all and we sat around a giant bowl to eat and washed down the Thieboudienne with bissap juice made with hibiscus flowers. We ate traditional style by sitting around the giant common bowl and scooped up the food with our hands. We also shared a baguette and had some brownies for dessert (not a traditional Senegalese dessert). Best meal I had so far in Senegal!

Two days later I was able to walk without any pain and set out to visit Goree Island off the coast of Dakar. The island is infamous as being the embarkation point for slave ships bound for the new world. Access by ferry cost 5000 CFAs (about $10) and takes about 20 minutes to get to the island. There were lots of tourists on the boat as well as shop owners and potential guides. Several ladies tapped me on the shoulder during our short voyage to invite me to visit her boutique and promised I would get a good deal.

We were met on the island by a swarm of 40 to 50 guides, a few dressed in official uniforms but most were not. My friend and I declined the many offers of assistance and set off around the island on our own. Since we got away from the guides and we were one of the first boats of the day we were able to walk around in freedom and peace. Many of the shopkeepers were still sleeping or setting up and we got to see how the current residents of the island lived. We saw lots of kids in school and others playing a soccer match in front of the government buildings. I enjoyed the colors and the narrow streets between the houses. Island life seemed pretty relaxed until the tourists invade, then its all-out combat.

The dilapidated fortress on the far end of the island was pretty impressive. The big guns (14 inch diameter barrels and 12-16ft long) are still in place but now people are living in or set up shop in the battlements. The facility would have been awesome when it was new. I thought it was interesting that in the modern fort on the island the guns were pointed out to sea, but on the old fortress, constructed in the days of the slave trade, the guns were pointed at the land. Both the new and old fortresses were constructed by foreigners to protect their trade.

Most of the shops on the island sold either jewelry (we saw some kids in a hut stringing beads on necklaces and bracelets) or art. The art ranged from carvings to large painted canvases. My favorite was the found object art, where the artist incorporated some random items into a piece of art. We didn't buy anything, but most people on the return trip to the mainland had either a sack of jewelry or a painting of some kind.

Saint Louis, Senegal. 19 July 2010.

Twelve days after I arrived in Dakar I was anxious to get out of the city and see more of the country. My mission was to see Africa and I was eager to get on the road! My friend John flew down from Germany to join me on my first trip out of the city.

My first trip out of Dakar was to drive north to Saint Louis. It felt good to break away from all the buildings and crowds and the countryside is beautiful. There hadn't been a lot of rain but most of the scenery was green. The worst traffic was just outside of Dakar where we were reduced to a lane of traffic going in opposite directions (from 3 lanes). Road construction slowed us even more, giving the street vendors ample opportunity to sell their wares. If you showed interest in an item they would walk along with your car for kilometers. Almost anything you wanted could be bought along the road.

Once we broke free from the rolling Walmart the road opened up and was smooth and in excellent condition. In every little village along the road there were several fruit or other kind of stands. Lots of mangos were on sale, as well as freshly butchered meat hanging in the little roadside huts.

When we finally got to St Louis four hours later we found the bridge to the islands was restricted to one-way traffic due to bridge construction. After a twenty-minute wait we finally made our way over the rickety, patchwork iron bridge into supposedly one of the nicest and most historic places in Senegal. Some guidebooks described Saint Louis as a classic French colonial town and showed pictures of clean streets and restored colonial buildings. What we found was nothing as described. It must have been several years since the last review because the islands were crammed full of rough brick huts, dilapidated buildings, and overflowing with people and trash.

I think the most disappointing part was discovering that there was no surf. I had brought two boards with me in the hope of surfing that afternoon but no such luck. The beach was also sprinkled with little purple jellyfish with long stingers. A local fisherman said the only time the waves were big was in the winter from December to March- then he asked for 2000 CFAs "to help feed his 3 kids." Maybe I'll come back then...

On the second day in St Louis, my friend and I toured a museum that exposed the history of St Louis, back to prehistoric times as well as the colonial period when St Louis was the capital of Senegal. It was interesting to see all the historical artifacts and some of the local art on display.

After the museum we returned to the beach in the middle of the fishing village on the adjacent peninsula. Our fisherman friend from yesterday was there as well and greeted us warmly. There was no surf again even though the sea was agitated from the strong onshore winds. After exchanging pleasantries and general conversation I asked our fisherman friend to show me his Pirogue (local fishing canoe) and explain to us how they fished in the area. Our newly minted guide excitedly led us down the beach and explained the different boats, fishing techniques, local species and many other aspects of his life as a fisherman in St Louis.

Our guide said he grew up on the peninsula and witnessed a huge decline in the local catch. Where 20 years ago the fisherman stayed relatively close to shore and caught as much fish as they wanted, now days they had to go far to sea to find fish. What made it worse, according to our guide, were the three large international fishing boats working the waters within sight of the beach. Also in the past the fisherman were able to follow the fish as the migrated to the north during the summer into Mauritania, but now Mauritania strictly enforces a fishing license requirement, which the fisherman guide said was very expensive. He also mentioned the recent killing of a fisherman in Senegal who was caught fishing in an aquatic reserve, expressing muted outrage that the fisherman was murdered instead of simply arrested.

Many boats were on the beach and our guide said most of the village wasn't able to fish until the fish migrated south again in the fall. He then took us to the fish processing plant by the new lighthouse which was under construction and now needed since the boats had to travel so far from shore to find fish. Adjacent to a large covered area that served as boat storage and the fish market was a huge outdoor area covered with large tubs and chopping table where the fish were washed, gutted, scaled and finned, then left in salt water baths for up to 15 days for preservation. The locals would keep the sardines and catfish for their own consumption but would sell all the shark and more valuable fish, which were then shipped to Dakar and other points. As the majority of boats weren't working, the fish processing area just stank in the sun, waiting for the return of the fish.

Walking back along the beach we passed five young boys playing with a smaller Pirogue, trying to launch it into the water. The guide explained that the boys were in training to become fishermen and were in a trade school right now, even though only being around 8 years old. He then expressed some regret that his three sons were not going to be able to be fishermen, but he was encouraged that they were trying to get an education to become something else because he did not see a good future for fishing. Our guide then led us off the beach into the village and among the several religious schools. The little kids sat in circles of eight in their brightly colored clothes with their instructors and sang songs and repeated the words of their teachers. Each group had children of roughly the same age and they seemed to be bubbly and giggly, full of joy.

Then we passed larger huts where older boys stood in the shade around motors and learning about mechanics or other skills. Our guide said that other students are sent away to learn other skills or for further education. There were some larger schools on the neighboring island, including a large music school, the fisherman said the locals from the fishing village didn't feel comfortable there and would go elsewhere for school or business. The island seemed dedicated for tourism or the military as there are several large hotels and a couple military garrisons (there were several gendarmeries on the island but I didn't see any in the village). The island is smaller and the streets are mostly empty, but the fishing village was the exact opposite with over 15,000 residents crammed into little huts and exploding with life on a narrow peninsula that separated the Senegal River from the Atlantic Ocean.

Everywhere we went on the island and peninsula we were surrounded by goats. There must have been two goats for every person, and it seemed like St Louis was a vacation village or resort for them as they were sleeping on the beach, wandering around the huts, in herds everywhere. Some boys would occasionally drive groups of goats along the beach or along the narrow paths among the huts, but for the most part the goats just hung out and enjoyed the warm sun and ocean breezes. Our guide said the goats were given as presents for marriage or other celebrations and were important as well to them for meat (but not milk or cheese- our guide thought the milk would not be safe). None of the goats had any markings to show if they belonged to anyone and the guide explained that they would use or butcher the goats as needed and if there were any disputes (if your neighbor complains you ate their goat) the problem would be taken to the village elders who would decide the issue and their word would be accepted and all would be settled and life would go on. Even though on the island a different form of government was established with a mayor's office and official government buildings.

As we came to the end of the tour we visited a lot where older men were working on the banks of the Senegal River finishing two new 30-foot long boats. They were painting the boats in bright red, green, blue, and white colors with stylish graphics and words and phrases in

Wolof and Arabic. When we tried to take pictures of their art the men started yelling and put their hands out for payment, but the guide calmed them and we quickly left the area. The guide pointed out that the wood from old boats was recycled and used in the construction of their huts and fences because they had a tradition if anyone was to die on a boat the boat would never be used again. He said there were many deaths and he reminded us of the large cemetery behind the fish factory. The guide added that since they had to travel so far now to find fish that if something were to happen they would drown as it was too far to swim to shore.

At the end of our nearly two hour tour we gladly paid our guide 7000 CFAs (approximately $14 USD) and thanked him for showing us a side of St Louis we would never had seen otherwise. Our guide said that this money would allow him to feed his family for almost three days (he considered about 30 people as his immediate family and they all chipped in to support one another and work together on their boat, fix the nets, process the fish, etc...). However, he only had one wife and three children of his own. After the tour my friend and I loaded up the Landcruiser and drove back to Dakar.

N'Gor Island, Senegal 23 July 2010

John still had a couple days left in Senegal before he had to return to Germany so we decided to visit N'Gor Island off the coast of Dakar and Joal Fadiouth further south along the coast from Dakar.

In order to get to N'Gor Island you have to take a pirogue, a long wooden canoe that can seat about 50 and powered with a 25 hp outboard motor. The trip takes about five minutes and costs 500 CFAs (about $1). You pay at the window, take your receipt to the life vest shack for your personal flotation device, and then sit on the benches and wait for the next pirogue. The boats run every 15-20 minutes and drop you off at one of two beaches (the pirogue alternates beaches). Upon landing you drop off your life vest and you will be greeted by the island welcoming committee, who will take you on a tour of the small village for a small fee.

We finally managed to shake our guide after about an hour (my friend bought him off with some cigarettes) and I was able to find the famous surf spots on the left and right of the island. On the left side of the island is "Mommie and Poppie" named after two large rocks and on the right side of the island is the break, immortalized by the surf classic "Endless Summer."

"Endless Summer" is an epic surf movie from the 1960s where two California surfers take off on an around the world surf adventure, trying to follow the summer and surf year round. The first place they land in Africa is in Senegal and they stay at the hotel that faces N'Gor Island and surf the breaks on the right side of the island in the film. They introduced surfing to Senegal and today the breaks are full of little kids who surf much better than me. There are several surf schools and N'Gor Island even has a surf camp (but it was closed when we visited) and the kids live mostly on donated surfboards left behind by tourists as they leave. The sport shop in Dakar City shopping center has about a dozen new boards for sale at prices comparable to the states- about $700 per board- which is 1/2 of what an average Senegalese makes in a year.

There were about a 1/2 dozen kids at each break, but the numbers began to swell as time passed. Most of the sets were thigh to waist high, but you had to know the breaks- especially at Mommie and Poppie, where you had to make a hard right turn or you were in the rocks. I think I need to hire a surf guide to take me around the area and show me the rocks in the water. I don't need any more urchin incidents.

The return trip on the boat is free. All you need to do is grab a life vest from the pile after the passengers disembark and you are back on the peninsula in five minutes. At a buck a trip its worth visiting the island every week- but I should try to find some surfers or a guide with a boat so I won't be jammed in with everyone else while holding my board.

Joal Fadiouth, Senegal. 24 July 2010.

The next day John and I visited Joal-Fadiout, a small historic town 114 km south of Dakar. It was about a 2.5-hour drive each way along pretty good roads. The worst traffic we encountered was leaving and returning Dakar, where the roads compress and street vendors mob the cars. Besides that, the roads were mostly open- the only traffic being taxis and trucks loaded with earth or rock. Joal is easy to find- you just follow the road from Dakar south until it ends.

At the end of the road there is a parking lot and a footbridge that leads to the island village. As soon as we got out of the car an "official representative" of the tourist association greeted us and explained how the tourism corporation worked. For 10,000 CFAs we could hire a guide for a 90-minute tour that included a pirogue tour of the mangroves and a small island, the cemetery, and the main island. They also offered guides who spoke several different languages. As it was my first trip to the area we decided to pay for the tour.

Our first stop was by pirogue to a small mud island 100 meters from the main island where the locals used to keep their grain in small thatched huts in the water. The idea was to protect the grain from the rodents by putting in on a hut on stilts. Whenever they needed their food, they would pole out to the island in pirogues. Since the water was so shallow around the main island, the pirogues were propelled by pushing through the water using a three-meter long pole (ala Venice). The guide also talked about their efforts to regrow the Mangroves as many had been harvested for firewood and destroyed in the process.

Next we poled out to the cemetery, which is famous for being one of the very few cemeteries in Africa where Christians and Muslims are buried side by side. Unlike the rest of Senegal, which is 96% Muslim, Joal Fadiout is 90% Christian and the main island is dominated by a huge catholic church. The cemetery is as well dominated by white crosses but still has Muslims plots among the Christians. The cemetery is dug into a hill of little white shells and people are still buried there today.

Our final stop of the day was the main island where we were greeted by the sight of pigs running around and mixed in among the goats and other animals. These were the only pigs I had seen in Senegal and the guide made sure to point out every pig he saw. It seemed our guide was related to every one of the 8000 inhabitants of the island and he took us to every gift shop there. We did stop at the Catholic Church and walked past a few small mosques during the tour. The guide said the religious leaders encourage peace by inviting each other to their religious festivals so the Muslims would come to the Christmas mass and the Christians would go to Ramadan. The most unusual part of the island for me was that the streets were made of seashells. Every inch of the island was covered with shells, not sand. Centuries ago the island was formed by generations of people throwing their shells in a pile, just like the cemetery. Kind of like living on a cool landfill.

Thies, Senegal. 30 July 2010.

After Joal Fadiouth John had to return to Germany and I spent the next couple days in Dakar researching my first big trip out of Senegal to eastern Africa and hanging out around the embassy. A couple days later I was off on my first Military to Military engagement at the

African Infantry School in Thies, Senegal. The Vermont National Guard had teamed up with the country of Senegal as part of the State Partnership Program and had sent two Infantry non-commissioned officers from a mortar team to participate in a mortar familiarization course.

We traveled to Thies together for the weeklong event and I introduced the American soldiers to a class of twenty Senegalese soldiers at the Infantry school. The Americans came prepared with pictures and PowerPoint slides to share how American infantry units employ mortars in combat. Both of the American troops had served in mortar crews in Afghanistan or Iraq and freely shared their experiences through the two interpreters who translated from English to French. Later the Senegalese soldiers took us to their mortar range and demonstrated how they set up and fired their mortars, running crew drills using 80mm and 120mm mortar tubes. The Senegalese mortar crews were proficient and enjoyed sharing their experiences from peacekeeping operations with the Americans.

Thies is the first big town outside of Dakar and the crossroads of two major roads in Senegal. There is a small airport outside of town, several businesses and international offices, some factories, and a large military training area. It's pretty laid back and definitely a lot calmer than Dakar. Food was pretty good and we found a lot of expats eating at "Big Faim," which has huge burgers (bigger than a softball) packed with two hamburger patties and your fries too.

The area around Thies is pretty flat with some dry riverbeds, lots of bushes, and some huge Baobab trees. It was interesting to walk around in the bush outside of town because the bushes were tall enough to hide the nearby buildings and you could quickly become disorientated with no distinct landmarks with which to navigate.

Even though Thies is only 70km from Dakar the trip takes around two hours due to all the congestion in Rufisque, where the autoroute from Dakar condenses into a small two lane road under construction and full of trucks hauling stuff into and out of the city. Often the large trucks will break down in the middle of the road, backing up traffic for hours.

People swarm the vehicles stuck in traffic selling everything from mangos to parrots. Others have called it "Walmart on Wheels" as you can buy underwear, lamps, rugs, phone cards, soccer balls, and so on. If you show interest in an item the vendors will follow you for the whole hour or so it takes for you to creep down the road.

Back in Dakar after the excitement of the week, the weekends seem like a ghost town. Downtown the streets are empty as all the street vendors and panhandlers pack up their shacks and head home for the weekend. The streets are nearly deserted and I can walk around in peace and not get hassled every 10 yards. A couple people walked up to me but didn't try too hard to sell their watches or phone cards. I think the people in the neighborhood are starting to recognize me and realize that I am not just a tourist passing through.

A cool sight downtown is the large Catholic cathedral. It is also surrounded by the catholic schools (elementary and high schools) where many of the more affluent Senegalese send their children.

A fun game I have started to play is to find the different embassies in the city. Today as I wandered the deserted streets I walked by Cameroon, USA, Lebanon, and Russia. Yesterday I ran by China, Ghana, Spain, and Saudi Arabia on my eight-mile run up the cornice and around the African Renaissance Monument. I'd love to take pictures of the different buildings and cool architecture but unfortunately, the guards at the embassies and official buildings get upset if you start taking pictures.

Before I moved to Senegal I lived in the small California coastal town of Monterey where the people were very laid back. Moving to the crowded extremely busy and aggressive city of Dakar was a shock to my system, especially as the people are very demanding in French and Wolof. Struggling to communicate in a new foreign language adds to the stress and I needed to de-stress with some surf therapy. Midweek after lunch I snuck out of the office and went to the beach. It was cloudy and sprinkling all morning but when I got to the Secret Spot the rain stopped. When I paddled out the clouds parted and sun started to shine.

The waves were beautiful, about waist high with occasional chest high sets. The outside larger waves were green, but inside they were black with shredded kelp. The closer you got the shore the thicker it was, to the point where it felt like I was pulling myself through a field of waist high grass. Still the conditions were pretty clean and if you took off in front of Chez Fatou (the restaurant/bar that faced the break) you could make the section and ride it in to the tiny sand patch beach.

It's amazing how much better I felt surfing. I was able to relax and try to figure out the breaks because for the most part of the two hour session it was just me and another local surfer, "Happy," in the water. Turns out that Happy is a local surf guide who works at the shop at the Secret Spot and he offered to take me around the area to all the breaks for 10,000 CFA per day. He said he even has access to a boat to get to some of the outer breaks.

At 3pm a group of 20 young kids walked up the beach with their surfboards and bodyboards and swarmed the breaks. The kids were pretty good with a couple doing aerials near the shore break.

I wore my Vibram 5 Fingers in the water and they worked great! I used my regular pair that I use for running or walking around and they worked fine in the water too. I just strapped them down a little tighter and they stuck to the board well and protected my feet when I got too close to the rocks. The only time I felt an urchin was when it hit the topside of my big toe, but the spines did not penetrate the fabric! I may look like a dork using my 5 Fingers in the water but I love them and they did a great job protecting my feet.

When I was in Monterey I took a PADI SCUBA course and earned my Open Water certification so I would be able to dive around the continent. In Dakar there are two dive shops and one, the Oceanium, is located near my apartment in Plateau so I decided to walk around to find it. As I walked down the road along the Presidential Palace that leads to the Petite Cornice I saw a European guy walking up the same road quickly away from a Senegalese guy who was standing on the corner. When the European passed me I could hear him muttering something in French and he wasn't too happy.

As I reached the corner the Senegalese guy advanced toward me with his hand out and asked in French if I spoke English, quickly followed by the same question in Portuguese. I responded in Portuguese but he couldn't carry on the conversation in Portuguese and dropped into French and broken English. The Senegalese dude introduced himself as "Camaro" and offered to show me around but I declined telling him I was going to the Oceanium, which was across the street, directly in front of me. Camaro said he had a boat too and he wanted to show it to me and be a boat guide for my friends, and me I figured why not? So I followed him down a flight of broken stairs to a couple shacks on the waterfront where his boat was tied up. His boat was just an oversized rowboat without a motor, but it was afloat in the water. He said he had taken many people on boat tours in his boat, even down to the Gambia and Guinea-Bissau.

Camaro then proposed a business deal- we would open an office in his name, I would correspond with Americans and other Europeans and get them to come down to Senegal and he would be their tour guide. I would sit in the office behind the computer and he would do all the work. As part of his plan he said that he had friends with large houses on the southern coast who could let the guests stay at their place- he had it all arranged, all I needed to do was start bringing the guests to him. Because I wasn't too excited about his business pitch, Camaro wrote down his cell phone number for me and told me to give him a call after I had thought it over. But, he cautioned me, he might not answer the phone because it was an older cell phone and it might be out of minutes. He then proceeded to pull an old brick Nokia cell phone out of a garbage bag he was carrying with him to demonstrate how old it was. He said not to worry, just keep trying the number and eventually I would get through.

After listening to a tirade of broken French and English about how the Lebanese controlled the tourist trade in Dakar and raped the openhearted Africans, I followed a trail between the burnt garbage pile and the red brick shacks to the Oceanium parking lot. Camaro didn't follow any farther into the Lebanese owned dive center, but waved from behind the garbage pile. At the Oceanium I met the owner briefly and he invited me to come back on Saturday or Sunday because they only dove three times a week: Wednesday, Saturday, and Sunday. He said they would provide everything and it would only cost me 18,000 CFAs (approximately $36). The boat went out twice a day- in the morning and the afternoon and they would go to different dive sites depending on your level of experience and the depth you wanted to go. As I had just completed my PADI Open Water Certification, they said they would take me out to a place that was 10 meters (about 33 feet deep).

As I exited the Oceanium by a different path, Camaro raced to catch up with me and started cussing and swearing about the Lebanese again and how he was cheaper and I needed to go into business with him. I kept walking and talking to him in French and listening to his stories of how good a guide he was. Camaro then went on to talk about his most famous client- President George W. Bush, and how he had taken him around and ended up in a bar drinking Vodka with former president.

Half an hour later I still couldn't shake Camaro, even though I had gone up stairs and through another neighborhood to get to the Place d'Independance. When he started to give me a broken history lesson on the Place d'Independance I had enough. I repeated for the fifth time "I don't need a guide. I live here- I have been here many times, leave me alone" and darted through traffic across the street. Only by starting to raise my voice did he leave me alone. I guess I should be happy that I didn't lose any money in the process.

As I wandered through the streets I was amazed at how the European tourists stuck out, usually by following some advice from a guidebook, so the women would have their purses tightly strapped to their chests. Most tourists already stand out by wearing the latest safari gear from REI or some other outdoor store with huge vents in the back of their shirts and nylon pants. The funniest and most obvious tourists even wear the old British safari helmets in the crowded streets of Dakar. The first time I recognized an African tourist (tourist from another African country) I was surprised, but it made sense- Dakar is a great city with lots of colorful history- Africans from other countries would want to visit here too.

I arrived in Dakar a month ago and have learned a lot in that short time. I still have a lot to learn (learning Wolof would help a lot!), but it was interesting to see an interaction between a Senegalese man and a white tourist (probably American from his clothes). The tourist wore khaki cargo pants, a black t-shirt, and wore Oakley sunglasses on his shiny white shaved head. The Senegalese man wore traditional clothes, not the usual dark blue jeans and t-shirt that most people wear in Dakar, but the baggy cotton pants with matching long shirt. I was far enough away that I couldn't hear the words, but I knew what they were both saying.

"My friend, welcome to Dakar. Are you American? Do you speak English?"

"Where are you staying? Let me show you my shop. Just look you don't have to buy anything."

"I have a gift for you to welcome you to my country. You don't have to pay anything- its a free gift. Here look at it, take it."

"Can you loan me some money as we are now friends?"

"Look, I gave you a gift, it would be rude not to give me a gift back."

"Let me see the other money you have in your wallet, I see you have other bills in there. Give me some."

Stupidly, the tourist had accepted the gift and had been coaxed into getting out his huge expedition-strength "hidden" wallet on the corner of busy street and given cash to the local. Eventually the tourist got angry and stormed away, a few thousand CFAs lighter. The Senegalese man watched him go, put the money in his pocket, and looked around for his next mark. I wasn't the only one watching this go down- it was just normal on the streets of Dakar.

2 TANZANIA, ZAMBIA, & MALAWI

Flying to Dar es Salaam. 17 August 2010.

It was cold and damp with a hint of smoke in the air when I got off the plane in Nairobi. I was unprepared for the chill in the early morning air- it was still hot even though it was raining when I left Dakar the night before. It never gets cold in Dakar. There is often less than a 10 degree Fahrenheit swing each day, so there is never any relief from the oppressive heat and humidity.

Kenya Airways was pretty good, better than many flights I have taken on American airlines in the past, with amiable stewards and decent food. I really appreciated the hot towels at the beginning of each flight. Since the flight was half full, I was asked to move to an exit row and sat by myself for the overnight flight. We did stop for an hour in Abidjan, Cote d'Ivoire to drop off and let on new passengers. So far none of the airports have had Wi-Fi, which would have been nice since neither of my cell phones work here. I will have to acquire a new sim chip and buy some minutes.

My good friend Brad met me at the airport and drove me out to his house out on the peninsula in Dar. For the next couple days he would be my host and traveling companion as we explored Eastern Africa.

Dar es Salaam, Tanzania is a very different town from Dakar. It's cleaner, not as crowded, and they drive on the left side of the road. Even the cars are right hand drive, like in England. The weather is great, nice and cool since its winter time and so far the people seem friendly. I like how the town is more spread out into neighborhoods instead of the harsh contrast of tall buildings in downtown Dakar surrounded by unfinished houses as far as the eye can see.

Dar es Salaam, Tanzania. 18 August 2010.

We started the day by traveling to the U.S. Embassy in Dar es Salaam to meet the American Defense Attaché and accompany him to the local navy base to deliver two Defender patrol boats to the Tanzanian Chief of Navy. The Defender patrol boats were 30-foot boats that could seat a crew of 12 and while it had a rigid hull it was surrounded by an inflatable chamber that increased its buoyancy.

The Navy Chief was friendly and gave us a quick tour of the large navy base with well-manicured lawns and sailors climbing over an obstacle course. The base, surroundings, and climate reminded me of visiting Pearl Harbor in Hawaii years ago.

After the morning visit to the base we went to the local Rotary Club Meeting held during lunch at a fancy hotel downtown. The meeting room was packed with local businessmen, NGO representatives, and even a couple people from the US Embassy. The group discussed working together to try to move from small projects with limited impact to larger programs that would support a community, taking a multi-faceted approach. The group discussed moving from unsustainable projects like donating beds to a hospital that the hospital couldn't maintain or giving an ambulance that the hospital that couldn't afford fuel to drive the ambulance. Some of the recommendations for donation were scholarships, vocational teams, or teacher training.

As we drove around Dar I noticed a number of vendors selling American style clothes along the side of the road. The t-shirts in particular stood out as many advertised events such as concerts or elections in the US. Brad told me that the locals called the clothes "dead Muzungo clothes" as they couldn't believe that people were donating items of such quality but thought it was more likely that these were the clothes stripped off dead white people and shipped off to Africa for sale. (In eastern Africa white people are referred to as Muzungos).

Pembe Island, Tanzania. 19 August 2010.

We went out for a nice 6.5-mile run this morning at about a 8 min mile pace. We ran mostly on the dirt roads in the neighborhood and by the beach just to glimpse the flat silvery water before turning back into the neighborhood of mansions. After a quick shower we drove out to an outdoor cafe and had a nice breakfast of croissants, orange juice, and eggs (with an extra bottle of water thrown in for me as I keep sweating for at least an hour after I run around here).

After breakfast I exchanged $300 for 450,000 Tanzanian shillings. I felt like a drug dealer carrying a huge stack of bills. They even gave me an envelope to carry all that cash.

Next we visited a shop to check the price of unlocking my iPhone 3GS and my friend's Blackberry Storm. The iPhone would cost $380 to unlock it, but the Blackberry was only $80 so I decided to keep my iPhone as it is. The shopkeeper offered to buy my iPhone for $800 and said that he buys them in Dubai for about $1000 and offered to buy as many I could bring in from the States.

After lunch we headed to the airport and caught a small 8-passenger plane to Zanzibar flown by a student pilot with ZanAir. The plane kept crabbing or fishtailing in the air and the landing was kinda sketchy, but we made it in one piece. The senior pilot had to keep reaching over to grab the controls to straighten out the aircraft. It was weird to sit right behind the pilot and watch the gauges over his shoulder.

Next we caught another 20-minute flight to the island of Pembe on a much larger18 passenger plane, this time piloted by two experienced pilots (and was much smoother). The flights only cost about $20 each and with taxes and the total round trip was less than $100.

On the ground in Pembe we had to wait 30 minutes for our ride to show up (they had thought we were going to show up another day the following week). Even though no one hassled us while we waited, a taxi kept orbiting the parking lot hoping we would change our minds and hire it to take us to a hotel somewhere. While we waited for our ride to pick us up from the airport a sweet little girl in a black headscarf kept circling around us and couldn't stop staring at us. The island was closed to all foreigners just 50 years ago and white folk were still a novelty. Little kids would cry out "Muzungos!" whenever they saw us.

Our driver, Sori, drove his little Geo Tracker equivalent fast, honking his horn to get people out of the way, exceeding 90 kph, driving on the left side of the road. Eventually after many near misses with bicyclists, cows, chickens, and carts we made it to the end of the paved road and drove the final kilometer over a rutted and washed-out dirt track to the Pemba Paradise Resort Hotel.

We arrived at the golden hour and I was amazed at the scenery- the silvery ocean, white coral cliffs, and huge baobab trees. The ambiance got even better with a purplish-pink sunset and the gentle sound of the waves rolling over the reef.

We were each assigned our own "banda" cabin with a palm-thatched roof with the basic essentials of a toilet, sink, shower, and a wooden bed. It wasn't a four star hotel but was good enough. Power was on until 11pm, when they shut off the generator, and didn't come back until 6am so it was a little warm without a working fan or an AC unit. Thankfully the constant ocean breezes kept the temperatures down.

Pemba and Zanzibar Islands, Tanzania. 20 August 2010.

This morning I woke up on the island of Pembe after a good night's rest in the middle of nowhere. In the morning light the small resort was more amazing than the evening before as I noticed the many banana trees, coconut trees, papaya trees, and baobob trees on the reef above a clear blue lagoon. It was low tide and the local villagers were wading throughout the water collecting squid trapped in the pool behind the outer reef. The women would bring the squid to the men sitting on the shore who were smacking the squid against the rocks, killing and tenderizing the squids for dinner. A worker at the resort explained that a local delicacy is fried squid in a tomato sauce.

After breakfast we drove into Chake Chake, the largest city on the island, and visited the Old Fort. Researchers have determined it was either an old fort or palace, but they weren't really sure. It has been turned into a museum of the history for Pembe and it had some old artifacts from the period when the island was settled by Omani merchants who pushed the natives off their land. The display also included Chinese pottery from the 15th century and had a model home that explained all the aspects of local life and all the different elements found in a home in Pembe.

Behind the Old Fort was a concrete basketball court and our guide explained that this was one of two courts on the island and the locals were pretty good, in fact, some were recruited to play basketball back in the states. Unfortunately no one was playing at the time.

We also drove down a narrow road, which also served as the local market and was swarming with people. Lots of different things were for sale, including sandals, used shoes, "dead muzungo clothes," fruits, vegetables, and fish. It was very lively and colorful, even though they didn't like how our drivers were forcing their way down the narrow lane.

In the past 24 hours on Pembe I had only seen 2 other groups of "muzungos," and that was when we had briefly stopped a government hotel outside Chake Chake. The muzungos were an old retired couple that was volunteering at the local clinic. They referred us to another group of Americans that they had heard of working at the police academy in the hills outside of town.

We asked our driver to take us to go see the Americans and we found them on the grassy slopes of high hills above Chake Chake that had a clear view over cinnamon trees to the ocean, working with a class of 30 police cadets. The two Americans were part of a US Army Civil Affairs team visiting the island for a couple days to work with the Pembe police force. When we found they were teaching CPR and first aid to the cadets who were paying fast attention and eager to experiment with chest compressions and applying bandages. I thought it was remarkable that the class of cadets was mixed male and female and they were applying bandages for abdominal and chest wounds to each other.

The cadets told me about the local legend of "Bobowawa," a giant bat with one eye that sodomizes bad people until they publicly confess their sins. Sometimes a grown man would come into the village and cry out what he had done wrong or others would confess by painting or writing on the walls in town. Later in town we found Bobowawa painted on a wall.

The majority of the residents of Pembe Island are Muslim and during the holy month of Ramadan when we visited everyone was fasting. As there were few muzungos or tourists on the island all the restaurants were closed during the day. However, we discovered there was a bus-load of Chinese tourists visiting when they showed up at our resort on the last day looking for food. They had heard rumors that we were being fed during Ramadan and came hoping to order food as well!

This afternoon we caught a twin prop plane back to Zanzibar where I jumped ship to spend the night in Stone Town and Brad continued back to his house in Dar es Salaam. I ended up at the Tembo House Hotel, a nice place on the water with two PADI dive shops around the corner. I signed up for the Bahari Divers drive trip for a two-dive package for $100 USD, one off a reef and the other an old shipwreck, including all equipment and lunch. However, I would have to find another way back to the mainland besides the plane, as you aren't supposed to fly within 24 hours of diving due to the risks of nitrogen expansion in the blood cells. Luckily there is a ferry between Zanzibar and Dar es Salaam that travels every day.

Bawe Island, Tanzania. 21 August 2010.

I woke up on Zanzibar this morning at a great hotel, which unfortunately was also full of swarming mosquitos. I ate breakfast on the beach in the shade of some coconut trees and watched a pod of dolphins swim by 20 yards away. After I checked out from the hotel I wandered around Stone Town and made my way to the port and bought my ferry ticket back to Dar es Salaam for 55,000 Tanzanian Shillings. I got to the dive shop at 8:30, selected my gear, and we were on the boat by 9:15 heading out to Bawe island, a 30 minute boat ride away.

The instructors wore shorty wetsuits over a full wetsuit to keep warm since it was winter in Tanzania, but the water was still 82 degrees Fahrenheit. I wore a 2mm shorty wetsuit, which was a huge improvement over the 7mm wetsuit I wore for my last dive in Monterey. The visibility was also much better at 25 meters in the Indian Ocean compared to the frigid kelp forests of northern California. For the first dive of the day we dove to 17 meters (about 60 feet) and swam around a coral reef for 34 minutes.

For the second dive of the day we rode out another hour to Fungu Reef and explored the wreck of a ship that sank in 1941 while laying telephone cable between the islands. The hull was still there and there were a lot more fish in this area. At times I was fully enveloped in a cloud of hand-sized blue and white fish.

We were back in Zanzibar by 1 pm and I wandered around the back alleys and narrow side streets that were flooded with tourists and vendors selling the same wares out of every nook and cranny. The old three to four story whitewashed stone buildings were aged gray and reminded me of photos of Moroccan cities. The air was alive with Arabic and Swahili. I felt like I was in a movie.

I was on the Sea Express ferry by 3pm and underway by 3:30. The heaving seas were pitching the twin hulled express shuttle violently so 15 minutes into the trip they distributed sea sick bags and within 45 minutes passengers were lining the rail or filling their bags. The trip lasted 2.5 hours and there were many miserable passengers that were happy to disembark in Dar es Salaam.

The cab ride from the port to my friend's house in Dar was interesting because I agreed to a cab ride with one person that spoke English very well, but he jumped out of the cab 5 minutes later and left me with a cab driver whose English was very poor. Before he abandoned the cab the driver gave him 5000 shillings, so I assume that his job was to set up the cab rides for those who don't speak English well for a cut of the action. The ride cost me 20,000 shillings so the driver made about 15,000 shillings for the 20-minute trip. We still had to stop and ask for directions a couple times, but it all worked out in the end.

Dar es Salaam, Tanzania. 22 August 2010.

This morning we got up early and met some people from the yacht club and went on a six mile run. We ran with two white South Africans and a Kenyan and managed about a 8 minute mile pace over the dirt roads and the small hills of Dar es Salaam. Immediately after the run we jumped in the truck and headed back to the house so I could get changed for church.

I took a cab to church and got there a couple minutes early and passed the time talking to the missionaries, a black elder from Zimbabwe and a white elder from South Africa. The branch is part of the Kenya mission and has about 70 active members. I was the only white person there and the services are conducted mostly in English. The elders said they were only allowed to teach in English, even though the scriptures are also printed in Swahili.

In Sunday school the lady teaching the class shared a Tanzanian parable about a frog and a snake. They had both gone to visit the hare to learn how to get smooth skin. The hare started to explain- get a pot of water and start it boiling, then take the water... At this point the frog said he got it and hopped away. The frog went home and boiled some water and jumped in and his skin became very rough. The snake stayed and listened to the rest of the instructions- take the water off the heat, mix in the medicine, then let it cool, then take a bath in the cool water. The snake stayed and listened to all the instructions and that's why it has smooth skin and the frog has rough skin. The moral of the story was to not rush off without getting all the instructions. If you jump too soon you may get the opposite effect.

After church we hung out around the house and later went to dinner at another friend's house. It was a pretty quiet and easygoing Sunday.

Dar es Salaam, Tanzania. 23 August 2010.

We mostly hung out in Dar today and took it easy. We got the hotel reservations set up for Lusaka and Victoria Falls in Zambia, and

Lilongwe in Malawi; and prepared our bags and snacks for the long train ride from Dar to Livingston, Zambia. The trip is expected to take 40 hours if the train doesn't break down, if it does break down this trip may take several days.

I also bought a new cell phone, a Samsung dual line touch screen phone for 400,000 shillings and got it hooked up for data so I can access Facebook, Twitter, the internet, and read my emails. I chose Vodacom for my service as it usually it costs 1 shilling per second in Africa, but a call to the States would cost six times as much.

After dinner we cruised out to a shopping center on the beach and enjoyed ice cream cones while we watched the sun set. Tanzania and Dar Es Salaam are amazing and very peaceful. I definitely want to come back for an extended stay in the future.

Tazara Train to Zambia. 24 August 2010.

We spent the morning packing and making final preparations. We headed down to the train station right after lunch in case the train decided to depart early, as it did on occasion. In the first class lounge we found a variety of people who had also arrived early to wait for the train. There was a missionary couple who lived in Zambia four hours from the nearest paved road, groups of tourists with huge backpacks, and several well-dressed Africans. We heard people speaking in a variety of languages and when Brad and I were able to respond in French, German, and Portuguese they accused us of being American CIA spies as most Americans can't speak any language other than English.

We boarded the Tazara train to Zambia at 15:30 and departed the train station at exactly 15:50 as scheduled. We bought all the bunks in a four-berth first class cabin on the train for comfort and to minimize the chances we would get stuck with bad company. When we had told others of our grand plan to ride the rails to Livingston most laughed or told us we were crazy. Some told us to look out for robbers or thieves and the one person who had taken the train years ago told us about how one of the bunks in his cabin had been used for "professional purposes" by prostitutes.

We were surrounded by muzungos in our first class car, except for the one cabin next to us which must have housed VIPs because police officers kept stopping in to say hi and talk in Swahili and they got fed before everyone else. Two cars up was the lounge car with a bar stocked with plenty of beer, sodas, and water. Beyond that was the second class cars with six berths per room, and in front of that the cattle cars with open seating and regular seats like on a plane. I think there were only three first class cars on the 20-car train with the majority of cars carrying economy passengers.

The scenery for the ride was amazing with distant mountains and little villages everywhere. Since we were on the express train we didn't stop as much, but we did stop occasionally and were instantly swarmed by locals selling bananas, plantains, fruits, and fried chicken. Four hours into our trip we stopped for 15 minutes to allow a huge group of tourists to dismount with their expedition size backpacks and join a safari group heading into a game park. German backpackers with their equally large backpacks immediately occupied their empty cabins.

Dinner was served in our cabin at 9pm. I had some chewy gristly meat with rice while Brad ate the fried chicken and rice. The meal wasn't half bad and only cost us 7,400 shillings. The steward cleaned the plates by holding them out the window and allowing the wind to blow off the residue.

I was surprised to see the number of fires burning in the countryside and even though we were miles from any towns the smoke was still thick in the air. The bright orange and red flames stood out in the pale moonlight. Luckily we had a full moon so we could still see some of the landscape as we clacked along in the dark night.

The nights on the train were surprisingly cold as we crossed the mountains in the dark and we hadn't packed any sleeping bags. At first we tried to resist, but in the end we reluctantly wrapped ourselves in some dirty old blankets that had been left in our cabin.

Tazara train to Zambia. 25 August 2010.

We crossed from Tanzania to Zambia around 6pm. There weren't any signs welcoming us to the new country, our only indication that we had actually crossed the frontier was a boy holding a handmade net attached to a post and a policeman standing next to him who was wearing a different uniform. The Tanzanian customs officials who had stamped our passports DEPART had gotten off at the previous stop and now the train was full of people calling out "change" as they roamed the corridors. We exchanged $100 USD for 420,000 kwachas and bought some samosas (triangle shaped pastries filled with mystery meat) from the vendors who swarmed the exterior of the train. I bought a visa for Zambia for $50 USD and since we were in First Class the customs officials came to our cabin to sell the visas.

This train trip through eastern Africa had been very enjoyable and scenic. A steward brought all our meals to our cabin and the washroom was just a few doors down from our cabin. If we wanted a drink or snack there was a snack bar in the next car. A couple police officers were in the last car of the train and they patrolled the first class cars, and had been more alert since we crossed into Zambia.

It's been hard to tear my eyes away from the window. The landscape has been awesome and ever changing. The villages have changed their shape and building materials (cement versus red clay bricks, tin roofs versus straw) and it was great to get a glimpse of people in their normal lives. In some towns the women were washing clothes in the creek and spreading them out to dry on the rocks, in another area some women had dug a pit in a dry riverbed and were using buckets to scoop up water to carry back to their homes.

It's also been interesting to see the brick making process as we fly by on the train. In one area people are mixing the clay and putting it into forms. Next to that another person is stacking the dried grey bricks into a tower with ports at the bottom and an open center area. In another area someone is jamming wood into the ports under the bricks and covering the tower of bricks with clay. When it's all sealed up, they light the fires under the bricks and start them cooking. Further down one can see some clay towers that were broken into and the reddish-orange bricks inside.

One great thing is that everywhere we go the children are excited to see us. If they can get close to the train when we stop they will run alongside it calling for water bottles or soap in Kiswahili. Whenever we stick our heads out the window they would cheer excitedly "muzungo!" Even in the countryside the kids would hear the train coming and run to the edge of the village and wave as we rushed by. Even some of the adults will break into a smile and wave if you wave at them.

Very few muzungos are left on the train now. Most had gotten off for a safari in a national park or in one of the larger cities before we left Tanzania. The missionaries got off the train around 4:30 this morning for a four-hour truck ride into the mountains to get to their compound. I think at this point the only muzungos left on the train are Brad and I and the Russians.

Another interesting aspect to the train is how it serves as the local marketplace and gives villagers in remote places an opportunity to sell their goods. The Africans in the car next to us have been on a shopping frenzy; at one stop they bought two huge sacks of potatoes, then at the next stop a huge sack of rice that must have weighed at least 20 kilos. They must travel this route a lot because sometimes people will walk right up to their window, talk a bit in Kiswahili then exchange the heavy sacks for some cash. Even at 3am, the locals are waiting for the train and are selling everything from chicken (live chickens) to sugar cane. In the larger settlements they even have the duty free shops with people selling cookies and perfumes.

Unfortunately some of the other great cross-border train routes have stopped operation and probably at a great loss to the local economies sustained by train travelers. I was hoping to take the Dakar-Bamako train but it has been out of operation for three years now. There are still some train services like the Rovos, which travels all over the continent, but at a luxury price. The trip from Johannesburg to Cairo would be amazing, but costs $45,000 for the "economy" ticket. I am very happy with my $50 USD (70,000 Tanzanian shillings) ticket.

Lusaka, Zambia. 26 August 2010.

After 55 hours we finally made it to our hotel in Lusaka from Dar es Salaam. The Tazara train made it to Kapiri Imposhi at 1pm, but then we had to get to Lusaka before we could rest. It was starting to feel like an episode of the Amazing Race.

Luckily we met a local lady who adopted us and helped us make our connections to Lusaka. She told us to call her "Aunty" and she said she would take care of us. She caught a cab with us from the train station to the bus station about 5km away, then she waited with us and caught a bus to Lusaka together, and then we shared another cab from the Lusaka bus station to our hotel before she went on to her home. She was very helpful when at the Kapiri bus station a local African started harassing us. She yelled at him to go away and called the attention of the security personnel in the orange vests when it was obvious that he was high and just wanted to cause a scene. Eventually the security guys took the troublemaker away and he started a fight. The last I saw of him was a circle of orange vests in a cloud of dust surrounding the guy on the ground. Besides that minor incident we had no problems at all on our trip.

Until we got to Lusaka we didn't see any other muzungos. The people on the small 24-passenger bus weren't really sure what to think about us. They were very nice and Brad shared his pretzels with the kids and although we were tightly packed together it was a nice ride. Once we got to the city and people started getting off the bus bedlam ensued, as one lady who had many large bags wasn't keeping track of them. When we got to her stop at the end of the trip she discovered she was missing a large bag and started yelling at the driver and doorman in Nyanja or some other local language. I couldn't make exactly what she was saying but it was clear she wasn't happy and held the bus people responsible. We quickly got into a cab and drove away before she made too big of a scene.

We experienced a mini-culture shock when we walked into the lobby of the four-star hotel. We had gotten used to being among the locals and all of a sudden we walked into a room with marble floors where Africans were a distinct minority, everyone spoke English, and drinks were $5.00 USD. After three days on the train we were black with soot and pretty ripe and I appreciated the hot shower, electricity, and wifi. There was even a large outdoor pool, but it was too cold to swim.

We indulged in a nice dinner at the hotel that cost 136,000 kwachas ($35 USD) each and featured a five-piece band that played western and local tunes but without any soul. An interesting part of dinner was seeing the fat old white men with beautiful black women, sometimes with two stunning women at the same time. By the end of the day I was worn out and crashed by 9pm local time. Somewhere on the train we crossed into a different time zone and I didn't realize it until dinner when we had to wait an extra hour for the restaurant to open for dinner at 7pm.

Livingston, Zambia. 27 August 2010.

I enjoyed la gross matinee this morning (sleeping in), until I realized that I was still an hour off due to the hour change. We had a great breakfast in the hotel and tried to find a flight to Livingston. Unfortunately, the guy at the hotel who helped arrange travel for the guests said that only flights available would cost $450 USD each way and the buses which would complete the distance before dark had already left for the day. The only other option to get to Livingstone by nightfall, where we had reservations for that night, was to rent a car with a driver. The hotel travel representative arranged a driver and car for $550 USD, but when the car showed up three hours later (two hours late) we found out that we had to pay an addition $100 for the drivers food and expenses.

We finally got on the road around 2:30pm for the 500km drive to the far end of the country through some very scenic country. We passed many little villages consisting of a circle of mud huts, sprawling lush green farms with irrigation and sprinkler systems straight out of the Midwest, and lots of big trucks carrying huge crude copper ore ingots from the mines. We also ran into lots of cattle and police check points every 50km or so along the road. For the most part the roads were in great shape and we were able to cruise comfortably at 130km/hr in our new Toyota Landcruiser Prado. That was until it got dark out and discovered the headlights didn't work. The last 30 km to Livingston were pure torture as we couldn't see the edge of the road and whenever we saw a car coming towards us we had to turn on our hazard lights so they could see us.

By the time we finally got to the Zambezi Sun we were worn out. We checked in, got some dinner at the $40 USD per person buffet and fell asleep to the sounds of a local African band singing off tune covers of Bob Marley- "don't worry about a thing... every little thing is gonna be alright."

Livingston, Zambia. 28 August 2010.

Since we got in so late the previous night we weren't able to check out the resort so immediately after eating at the enormous breakfast buffet we set off exploring. The Zambezi Sun is set up like a family resort with African drummers and dancers in reception, lots of sculptures of animals (giraffes, crocodiles, hippos), and many of the real animals roaming the area. The large semicircular pool is the center of the resort and surrounded by apartment style buildings. Our room looked out over the Zambezi River above Victoria Falls and occasionally baboons or other small monkeys would climb up to our room and jump from balcony to balcony. There were signs everywhere to remind you to be careful with the wildlife: "close your windows so the baboons don't get in your car" or "watch your kids so the crocodiles don't eat them."

The resort also has an adventure center so visitors can book a walking or Segway safari, go white water rafting below the falls, fly-fishing, or bungee jumping from the Victoria Falls Bridge. Most of the trips cost about $120 per person and my friend tried to schedule a fishing trip but the adventure center couldn't find a guide for the same day. I ended up walking out onto the Victoria Falls Bridge to watch the bungee jumpers and continued on to Zimbabwe while Brad took a nap in the room.

After clearing immigration I walked another two kilometers to the small resort town of Victoria Falls but along the road at regular intervals I would run into a street vendor. Each street vendor had a specific territory about 200 meters long and as I walked into each area the guy would walk up to me and try to sell me 100,000,000,000 (100 trillion) dollar notes. As I reached the end of his territory he would stop and another guy would greet me and begin again to try to sell me the same hyper-inflated currency notes. I couldn't tell if they were real or not as they had no seals or special markings like those of the neighboring currencies so I didn't buy any, despite the efforts of dozens of vendors.

When I finally made it to my destination, a huge hotel at the edge of town, I registered for the Victoria Falls Half Marathon to be held the next morning. They were also running the full marathon and each event cost only $35 USD in US currency. The people running the event and most of the patrons were white, but there were several thin and fast looking Africans trying to register as well. The races only cost $10 for the locals.

After I walked back across the frontier to Zambia I found Brad still trying to find a fishing guide and we ate some lunch at the poolside restaurant. Then we went on a short hike to Victoria Falls, an amazing waterfall where the wide Zambezi river plunges over 300 feet into a narrow canyon creating a huge column of mist that can be seen from miles away in the early morning light (its harder to see at midday). I was much more impressed by Victoria Falls than Niagara Falls, which I visited three months ago before moving to Senegal. There were some local Africans fishing in waist-deep water just yards from the edge and others that offered to guide you across the river just a hundred yards from the edge to Livingston Island. Both ideas seemed too risky for me as there would be no way to survive a trip over the falls and apparently dozens of people go over every year.

My favorite view of the falls was from the Knife's Edge trail and bridge just below the falls to a huge ridge that is perpetually soaked from the mist. There was a chain and a occasional railing to help you negotiate the slick surface, but there were plenty of areas where if you slipped there was nothing to stop you from enjoying a quick free-fall to the rocks below.

The Knife's Edge is also home to many baboon families who live out of the garbage cans. I quickly discovered that they don't like a camera flash when I took a picture of a baby clinging upside down to her mother's belly and the daddy came after me and chased me up the trail.

On the way back from the Knife's Edge we ran into a couple Zambians who quizzed us on our trip and what we were doing in Zambia. The two Zambians were strong and well dressed and insisted on getting a group photo before they would let us go. Perhaps my visit to Zimbabwe and crossing the border had inspired the Zambian secret police to investigate me. It does seem odd that two Americans had just taken a train, bus, and car to cross two-thirds of the way across the continent just for fun.

After exploring we hung out at the pool and had a couple drinks before heading to dinner at a restaurant. The British style wood paneled restaurant was packed with mix of Africans and muzungos who were cheering loudly for Manchester United on a enormous nine square meter screen. The food was fantastic, I ordered the grilled crocodile, which didn't taste like chicken, but like nothing else I had tried before.

Livingston, Zambia. 29 August 2010.

This morning, according to the immigration logbook, I was the second person across the bridge into Zimbabwe and by the time I had cleared immigration I could see the marathoners running down the hill from the start towards me. They were moving fast and I had to sprint up the hill to the start of the half marathon. Luckily there was also a wheelchair division before my race so I still had time to stretch and take a couple energy gels before the half-marathon race started.

There were about 300 people lined up for the half marathon and about three-quarters of them were white. Every race number had your country of origin annotated and I saw Canadians, Swedes, South Africans, and many white Zimbabweans. Once the gun fired to start the race, the black Africans took off like rockets and the white folk plodded after. We ran down the hill from the Ecobank, through customs and immigration, then out on the Victoria Falls Bridge to the Zambia gate before we turned around and ran back across the bridge to Zimbabwe and then along the Zambezi River into a park. I saw lots of baboons in the forest and every half-mile or so there would be a soldier or policeman with a rifle ready, I suspect with a mission to protect us from the animals. You had to keep an eye on the road to avoid the frequent large elephant piles on the road.

The African runners were impressive, especially when you considered their gear. I was passed by guys wearing clear plastic sandals, dress shoes, and many were shoeless. The guy that was most remarkable to me was wearing thick neoprene dive boots and blew by me like I was standing still. I don't think I passed any Africans during the race but I was just happy to be running in Africa.

There were many aid stations along the route (about every 2-3 km) handing out small sacks of water or an electrolyte drink. I thought the sacks were a huge improvement over the cups of water you usually find on the racecourse. I was able to bite and tear a small hole in a corner of the sack and squeeze the water into my mouth as well as fold the sack over and run with it for a while in my hand without the fluid sloshing out. Some of the aid stations even had sprinklers to run through to cool off.

Around the 10k mark we turned around and ran into and up the hills outside of Victoria Falls. Only near the end of the race did we come back into civilization and finished in a nice athletic compound by running around a polo field. I was worn out by the end and finished in 76th overall with a time of 1:46 for 13.1 miles. I got a nice finishers medal, a T-shirt from the beer sponsor of the race, and a bottle of warm water. Within 10 minutes of my crossing the finish line for the half marathon the winner of the full marathon strode into the field and won with a time of around 2:25. He was flying and I didn't see anyone behind him, I figure he beat his rivals by several minutes.

After stretching a bit, I bummed a ride back to the race start in the back of a pickup truck and walked back across the bridge into Zambia. After a quick shower, Brad and I drove back to Lusaka (I slept in the back of the car) and got to the hotel in time for dinner and a good night's sleep.

Malawi. 1-6 September 2010.

After spending a couple days in Zambia we flew north to Lilongwe, Malawi. The first place we passed on our way from the airport to Lilongwe was the school that Madonna was building and later several Chinese construction projects. The Chinese government had just built a new parliament building for the Malawian government and had a giant space dome shaped hotel in progress.

We stayed at the Sunbird Capital Hotel the first couple nights in Lilongwe, which was located across the street from the new Chinese hotel and in a central location. The Sunbird Capital was adequate but ominous as when we checked in there was a couple at the front desk complaining that their backpack with passports and credit cards had just been stolen from their room. The place was dingy, worn out, and just didn't have a good vibe. Brad said it reminded him of Soviet bloc hotel, cold and mildewy with no soul.

Brad and I were impressed by the cleanliness of downtown Lilongwe, the streets were clean and the curbs painted, and many of the shrubs and lawns in the public areas were well maintained. The second day of wandering around the city we ran into a work crew of prisoners closely guarded by several police who were sweeping and cleaning the roads. The prisoners stopped us and asked where we were from and welcomed us to their city. The police nodded and said "Hi" and we continued on our way.

In Malawi there wasn't an American Defense Attaché in residence but the U.S. Embassy did provide some assistance through programs such as PEPFAR and the Global Health Initiative, spending over $220 million USD in on HIV/AIDS prevention in one year. We also met with the American Centers for Disease Control in Lilongwe, which was also focused on HIV/AIDS prevention work and operated a lab in the city. The CDC worked with and trained local clinic staff and was also tracking drug resistance. The doctor who met with us explained that while there was a medical school in Malawi many of the doctors left after graduation, lured away by higher pay and better living and work conditions elsewhere, resulting in significant "brain drain." Trained nurses also followed the doctors to England or other Anglophone countries, resulting in a greater population of Malawian doctors in Manchester than Malawi.

Malawi is one of the few places in Africa where the US Centers for Disease Control (CDC) maintains a permanent office and we were able to meet with the director. One of the main focuses of the CDC was prevention, treatment, and care of HIV/AIDS as Malawi has a high prevalence rate. The United Nations organization covering HIV/AIDS, UNAIDS, estimated that in 2013 over 1 million Malawians were living with HIV and 10.3 percent of the population over age 15 were living with HIV. The CDC was also tracking other diseases, hemorrhagic fevers, and the Lujo virus, particularly the linkage between Tuberculosis and HIV. Malawi also was one of the few African countries that trained doctors but was also suffering from "brain drain" as many of the newly trained doctors fled Malawi for higher paying jobs in England or other English speaking places in the world.

Another significant issue mentioned by the CDC was the

unsustainability of clinics and programs operated by non-governmental organizations (NGOs). Most NGOs set up a health related program with a three to five year program life and once the program was complete the NGO would pack up and leave. Subsequently the services that the community came to depend on would also stop. This was a critical problem in the case of administering antiretroviral treatment because patients become dependent on the drugs. If treatment is stopped the patients often quickly deteriorate and die.

A theme that we were starting to find as we traveled was that while NGOs were doing good work they weren't necessarily working with anyone else and often duplicated the efforts of the government or other groups. If an NGO provided the same services but at a higher quality the people would stop going to the government provided service and the government service would shut down. The NGO problem was exacerbated by the short program life, with many programs only enduring three to five years then having to close due to funding and scope of project issues. In effect, NGOs could cause a government provided service to terminate and then leave a gap in services when the NGO program closed a few years later. As a relatively stable English speaking country, Malawi had more than its fair share of NGOs and potential problems if funding was terminated.

One day for lunch we asked a taxi driver to take us to a relaxing place for lunch and he delivered us to the Sanctuary Lodge just a couple blocks away from the Capital Sunbird. It was like walking into the Garden of Eden- it was clean, quiet, and calm in a nature preserve surrounded by green trees. As we ate lunch on an open veranda I was amazed by the lush verdant tranquility. We immediately checked out of the Sunbird Capital and moved into the Sanctuary Lodge and stayed in a cabana that had Wi-Fi access, but no television.

The next day we decided to drive to Livingstonia on Lake Malawi and rented a VW Polo sedan (like a VW Jetta) from Avis Rental Car. Originally we had reserved a SUV for the trip but when it came to pick it up it was already rented to another customer. Unfortunately we couldn't find a good map and ended up navigating off the map in the Lonely Planet guidebook and missed the turn for route M14 to Lake Malawi (the road wasn't marked). We ended up traveling 20 km up route M1 and turning on the only paved road we could find outside of Lilongwe. The asphalt quickly turned into a dirt road but since the dirt road was in good condition we decided to keep going. The road paralleled a new road construction project and started winding into the mountains and 30 km later we arrived in the town of Dowa.

We found ourselves on the map again and saw that the road we had followed, the route M7, continued south and eventually linked up with the M14 to Livingstonia so we decided to push on. The road south out of town wasn't as nice as the previous road and soon we discovered as we climbed over a ridge it quickly became more and more rutted. As we pushed on the car scraped bottom a couple times, but we continued in the hope that the road would soon improve again. The VW Polo wasn't made for dirt road travel (no 4x4 vehicles were available when we went to rent a car) and after about 6km and 30 minutes of nail-biting travel later when we almost high centered the vehicle we decided it was time to turn around.

After a dicey nine-point turn on the side of a steep cliff in the middle of nowhere and out of cell phone reception we started to make our way back up the hill to Dowa. Looking back up the road we had just descended the route looked like a staircase of short rutted ledges. We almost didn't make it out- several times we scraped over rocks, ledges, and drop offs and turned to each other and said "We shouldn't have made it this far- what were we thinking?" The people in Dowa looked at us like we were crazy when our dusty faces rolled back through town. 60 km later we were back in Lilongwe and were able to find the M14 to Livingstonia.

As we cruised along the M14 we passed the point where the M7 connected and the road looked like hell. From our vantage point on the paved road, the dirt road we tried to descend had several large drop offs and many sections where the trail narrowed to a single track. There was no way the tiny VW Polo could have made it through.

On the approach to Livingstonia we saw more and more mosques and the people began to dress more conservatively. We saw several people wearing suits even though it was just a Thursday afternoon. In the rest of the country and in the region we had observed most people dressed casually, often in a t-shirt and pants so the suits seemed out of place. Perhaps the suits were a local custom or there was a special occasion that day in Livingstonia. I would have to (and would like to) spend more time in the place to see what is normal behavior.

Livingstonia was an average town with only a few paved side streets and we quickly drove through to the lake and ate lunch at Sunbird Livingstonia on the beach. The plush resort and swaying palm trees on the sandy beaches on the blue lake was a beautiful sight. The food was good and it was nice to relax on the shores of Lake Malawi after almost being stranded in the mountains.

We eventually tore ourselves away from the relaxing scene and drove back to Lilongwe without any further incidents. We did stop to check out what the kids were selling on side of the road: smoked mice on a stick. The kids said they caught the mice in the surrounding fields and smoked them over a small fire. They claimed it was a local delicacy but the mouse-kabobs smelled rancid and the smell lingered in the car for several miles even though we only took pictures.

Later that night the Sanctuary Lodge held a silent auction as a fundraiser for a local wildlife refuge. A local artist contributed 40 wildlife paintings and a large crowd had gathered. I was quickly outbid on my favorite painting of an elephant crossing a river and most paintings sold for over $300 USD.

The best food in our experience in Lilongwe was at the Italian restaurant on the polo fields. The Malawian elites seemed to agree as the night we ate there had Maseratis and Bentleys in the parking lot. Its always interesting to go from the villages in the countryside where the people have nothing and sleep in the dirt to the capital with luxury hotels, fine dining, and polo fields.

Nairobi, Kenya. 6 September 2010.

Flying back to Dakar from Lilongwe I had to stay overnight in Nairobi, Kenya to wait for the connecting flight. I was able to make a reservation at the Hilton and a shuttle picked me up from the airport and carried me to the heart of Nairobi in relative ease. The hotel was nice but only had Wi-Fi in the lobby or the Resident Lounge .

I had a wedge shaped room on the ninth floor of the cylindrical tower overlooking the city. It was a nice view and later that evening a rainstorm blew in and drove away all the people on the streets below. I was surprised at how crowded the city was for Saturday evening.

The next day the Kenyan Airways flight back to Senegal was scheduled to depart on time, but boarding was delayed several times. When we were finally ready to depart two hours late one of the passengers was suddenly too sick to continue and the stewardess called for a doctor to come to the plane. Since we were now delayed more than three hours we had to offload the plane and wait for a new flight crew to arrive.

By now it was lunchtime and the airline brought all of us (over 100 passengers) up to the airport executive restaurant and served us lunch. Three hours later we were finally able to load again and get underway.

I arrived five hours late in Dakar to a pounding thunderstorm and made it back to my downtown apartment by 11pm.

Dakar, Senegal. 9 September 2010.

Back in Dakar and recovered from my eastern African adventure, I went exploring with a group of friends and visited the Carmel Market in downtown Dakar. The center of the market is a huge pavilion with several inner rings of vendors under the vaulted roof, selling everything edible that you could imagine. The vendors were arranged in sections with produce in the outermost ring, then meat in the middle ring, and finally seafood in the center of the pavilion. It was amazing to see all the vibrant colors of the fruits and vegetables stacked over a meter high. The colors, smells, sounds, and pressing crowds were almost overwhelming.

The market was packed with people rushing to buy last minute items to break their Ramadan fast, but also the vendors were in a hurry to make a deal as the following day was a holiday to celebrate the end of Ramadan. Since we were in a large group of Americans the vendors tripled their regular asking prices. After much negotiating I was able to negotiate the price of a 18" by 24" giraffe carving from 120,000 CFAs down to 20,000 CFAs (from $240 USD to $40 USD).

Dakar, Senegal (Western Accord Planning Conference). 13-15 September 2010

For two days representatives from the Economic Community of West Africa (ECOWAS) met in Dakar to plan a multi-lateral military exercise to be held in the summer of 2011. The basic plan was for one company from each country: Senegal, the Gambia, Guinea-Bissau, Guinea, and Burkina Faso to travel to Senegal with their weapons and military vehicles, stage, and then attack a fictional enemy. The exercise was scheduled to take place at the military training range in Thies and the U.S. military was to assist with transportation, logistics, as well as provide U.S. troops for the coalition.

The official mission statement was: USAFRICOM conducts exercise Western Accord 11 (WA11) in Senegal with the ECOWAS Stand-by Force (ESF) in order to enhance the ESF's ability command and control, deploy and sustain forces in support of stability operations. In support of the exercise the U.S. was also going to send to Thies a team of U.S. military dentists, doctors, engineers, and veterinarians to work with the ECOWAS medical teams and engineers.

The plan was for the teams to go into Thies and the surrounding communities to provide medical assistance and repair clinics, schools, and other infrastructure that needed assistance. This would replicate the mission of winning the support of the local community and providing assistance to the local population, part of winning the hearts and minds.

The big challenge for this regional exercise was that not all members of the regional economic community trusted each other and not all countries had the same resources. Due to some countries supporting insurgent forces in neighboring countries relations among some of the ECOWAS partners was a little tense. Some countries were also unable to provide airlift to Senegal for their troops participating in the exercise so they usually turned to the U.S. to request logistics support. However, part of the exercise was for the ESF to figure out how to self-deploy themselves without external assistance and using only assets internal to the ECOWAS countries. This was a challenge as many of the countries that possessed air forces lacked operable aircraft and adequately trained aircrews.

☐

3 LIBERIA & GHANA

Monrovia, Liberia. 20 September 2010.

I flew all morning, leaving Dakar at 1am and after a five-hour layover in Accra, arrived in Monrovia at 1pm. I flew Air Nigeria and the service was great- I was pleasantly surprised with a gift bag with free socks and a toothbrush. It was all still marked Virgin Nigeria (Air Nigeria recently broke away from the Virgin family to become a separate airline) but the aircraft was still very clean and the staff was professional.

Flying out of Accra towards Liberia we flew over some awesome looking long surf breaks but the water as we approached Monrovia turned a nasty dirty brown with no waves. At Roberts International Airport I met up with Brad again and another friend Natasha. Like many African airports, Roberts International Airport is an hour by car from the capital city over pitted roads and through heavy traffic.

For dinner we ate at the Golden Beach restaurant on the beach just meters from a decent break. Waves were waist to chest high and the water looked pretty clean but I didn't see any surfboards and the shops in the area were limited to the bare necessities- no luxury items or stores around here. One nice thing was that I didn't have to change any money, as the places I visited listed all their prices in US Dollars and gave change in US Dollars too.

We stayed with Gwen from the U.S. Embassy as she lived alone in a large house near the Embassy. She was our host for our four-day visit to Liberia and would show us around the country.

Monrovia, Liberia. 21 September 2010.

Heavy rains throughout the night flooded the roads this morning- I should have brought my Gore-Tex rain jacket. Today we drove around in my Gwen's Nissan Patrol with a snorkel kit and had a blast plowing through the 2-3 feet deep puddles on the road.

Most of the roads aren't paved so we had to use the Patrol's four-wheel drive capabilities to get through some deep sand too. We checked out the port and a city beach, which was covered in trash washed in by the heavy storm overnight. Part of the port was blocked by sunken ships sitting on the bottom of the harbor left over from the civil wars. The broken off masts or part of the hulls jutted out of the water and made a large portion of the harbor unusable.

We visited a well intentioned but poorly executed boat ramp built with U.S. government funding near the port for the nascent Liberian Coast Guard. The ramp was near a pier but instead of sloping gently to the bottom of the harbor there was a two-foot step up to the ramp and a three-foot drop off at the other end into the harbor, making it completely unusable. The U.S. Government also constructed a boathouse near the pier, which consisted of a couple shipping containers stacked on top of each other. One of the lower containers functioned as a mechanics shop for small engine repair and another container stored the rigid hull inflatable boats (RHIBs). The upper container was a crude office space that overlooked the pier and boat ramp. The U.S. Embassy was working with the Liberian government to train sailors from the Liberian Navy for the unique role of the Coast Guard and had provided several RHIBs.

UN vehicles were everywhere in Monrovia. The locals rode their little 100cc motorbikes around or drove their crumpled taxis, but most of the people simply walked. As part of the peace deal to end the long civil war in Liberia many of the former combatants received a lump sum payment. Most of the bikes on the road were purchased by ex-combatants and many are used as moto-taxis or for delivery services.

We saw an example of a moto-taxi being used as an ambulance when a vehicle accident happened 10 meters ahead of us in a crowded shopping area (intersection of a couple roads and many road-side shacks and vendors on foot). A car hit a moto-taxi and was still on top of the bike while an unconscious and bleeding young woman was being set into the arms of the rear passenger on a moto-taxi. The crowd had just pulled the driver through the window of his car onto the muddy ground where the people closed in a circle around him and began to beat him. My friend driving the car said mob justice is the only justice in Liberia. People take matters into their own hands because what little law enforcement is around is completely ineffective.

Monrovia, Liberia. 22 September 2010.

No rains today, but there were still seas of muddy water throughout Monrovia. We forded the seas in our lifted SUVs to visit the UN offices in the morning.

The view of Liberia from the perspective of the United Nations Mission in Liberia (UNMIL) was as gray and overcast as the weather. As we toured their operations center they were receiving reports of weapons seizures and of a riot at a checkpoint caused by a motorcycle that tried to run a police checkpoint where they were shaking down travelers for bribes. When the police shot the motorcyclist the mob attacked the nearby police station, looted the station, and beat the police.

Despite having nearly 8500 UN troops on the ground and attack helicopters on standby it seemed that UNMIL was responding on a daily basis to crises across the country. While the disarmament program had retrieved most of the assault rifles from the population, Liberians had improvised weapons that were being used in attacks as well as in self-defense. UNMIL was meeting weekly with the AFL and Liberian police to coordinate actions and facilitate interaction. Overall security was improving and the biggest threat seemed to be from criminal gangs of less than 12 members or traffickers. Traffickers were moving drugs, cars, rubber, timber, and diamonds. A major concern were the rebel groups that had fled Liberia into neighboring Cote d'Ivoire with reports of more than 2000 rebels on the border waiting for an opportunity to return to Liberia and destabilize the country again.

After the UN meeting we drove across town via the red light district (named for the blinking red traffic light that had long ago broken and had been stolen) enroute to the Firestone plantation. The red light district was slammed and overflowing with people, cars, motorcycles, and mud. It took a while to crawl through the slippery mess but it was interesting, as always, to watch the people in the colorful market.

Liberia is famous for its rubber plants and today we visited the Firestone Rubber Plantation near Roberts International Airport. It's a huge place that is a community unto itself with schools for the children of the plantation workers, a supermarket, health clinics, post office, and several housing areas. The rubber trees are the main attraction, all planted neatly in orderly rows, like corn in the Midwest.

The trees are planted in groves and take about seven years before the new plants start producing rubber. Once mature, the rubber trees produce for about seven to ten years then the production drops and the trees are of little use to the plantation. Due to the war many trees are over 15 years old and aren't producing very much anymore and need to be cleared for the planting of new trees. One solution that is being explored by the government is to collect the old trees and burn them as biofuel in a power plant since there is a great need for electricity in Liberia.

The system for collecting the rubber from the trees is pretty simple. The bark of the tree is cut or perforated to allow the sap to come to the surface and collected in a cup. The process is similar to the maple syrup process back in New England. The rubber sap is gathered by workers and brought back to the collection point, processed, and shipped out.

To wrap up the day we visited the U.S. troops mentoring and training the Armed Forces of Liberia (AFL). Following the civil wars that ended in 2003 the U.S. government volunteered to recreate and train the Liberian military and the UN decided to train the Liberian police force. The former military was dismissed in a lengthy disarmament, demobilization, and reintegration program and a new recruitment program was established in 2006 where recruits were accepted from around the country and vetted for human rights abuses in their home villages and surrounding areas. Once accepted into the force, the U.S. military trained the recruits focusing on infantry skills and incorporated human rights training and respect for civilians in the curriculum.

By 2010 the 2000 soldiers of the AFL had completed their basic training but still did not have free access to their weapons, which were secured by U.S. contractors. The AFL had developed its own officer corps but was still led by a Nigerian colonel and sergeant major, a remnant of the ECOWAS peacekeeping and stabilization force that put down the civil war in 2003. The U.S. military advisors had developed a plan to transition access to the weapons and retire the Nigerian leaders within the next year if all continued to go well.

The next challenge for the AFL was that the five year contracts of the first batch of Liberian troops that started training in 2006 were about to expire and the AFL would soon have to start recruiting and training replacement troops for those that would decide to quit the army after their initial tour. A squad of U.S. Marine recruiters and drill sergeants had recently been deployed to Liberian to assist with the development of recruitment and training program.

The big question that the U.S., UN, and Liberian leaders struggled with was why is there an army in Liberia? Did they really need one? Currently the AFL was made up of one brigade of 2000 soldiers but their mission was vague. There was no air force and they were filling more of a National Guard role responding to natural disasters and providing community service. The Liberian military leaders said they wanted to support elections, participate in peacekeeping missions, support civil authorities, and provide controls. As a sovereign country, Liberia could do as it pleased with its military but they also had the responsibility to pay for its military. The more military capabilities it added would increase the cost burden on the country's limited resources.

This was going to be a challenge for Liberia as they didn't field the costs of standing up the new AFL. The U.S. provided training was presented at the level of support provided to U.S. soldiers with three hot meals a day, barracks/housing with electricity, new boots and uniforms for every soldier, and hot running water. Most people in Liberia don't have these things and the AFL became accustomed to standard of living above the general population. It will be very costly for the Liberian government to continue to provide these services and a significant drain on the national budget.

Monrovia, Liberia. 23 September 2010.

The day began at 0630 in the pouring rain driving the Nissan Patrol 4x4 from Monrovia to Buchanan. The roads were great until 17km past the airport when the smooth Chinese made road came to an abrupt end and the bone jarring torture began. We covered 150 km in five hours as the rain gradually stopped and the sun came out.

About half way into the trip we reached an old rusty iron bridge under repair and had to wait for an hour while the bridge was put back together. Heavy traffic had pushed the 1/4 inch steel plates off some of the iron girders over the swirling mocha river so a work crew was spreading out the plates and welding them to the girders.

The bridge work was being done by a maintenance crew from Liberian Agriculture Company (LAC), a rubber company located outside Buchanan and competitor of Firestone. Later that day we visited LAC and toured the plantation. Our guides told us that LAC had agreed to maintain the roads since all the rubber they produce has to be trucked to Monrovia over the same road in semis carrying 20-foot trailers weighing several tons each.

The LAC plantation was pleasant, but the rubber tapper villages and schools weren't as nice as the Firestone plantation and recently the workers protested at the LAC headquarters to demand benefits comparable to Firestone. In the past month the white manager of the plantation had been ambushed and killed by an angry mob and the rest of the expatriate workers were concerned for their safety. Before the ambush local politicians had gone on the radio complaining about LAC abuses of the workers and urged the workers to get revenge and take over the plantation. During the ambush someone cut down several large (over 50m tall) trees blocking the roads. The tall trees had trunks several feet in diameter and were dropped in groves where it was impossible to drive around the fallen trees. Unfortunately, UN and other security forces were not equipped with chainsaws so they were unable to remove the roadblocks and reach the plantation.

After the tour of the Liberian Agriculture Company rubber plantation we drove back to Buchanan to check out Buchanan Renewable Energy (BRE). They harvest the rubber trees that are too old to produce rubber anymore, chip them onsite, and truck them to the port in Buchanan. At the port the wood chips are loaded on boats to Europe where the wood chips are burned as fuel instead of coal. We walked among giant piles of wood chips over 50 feet tall and hundreds of yards long.

Monrovia, Liberia. 23 September 2010.

As we explored Liberia we had heard many interesting stories from our driver and the locals we met. Some of the stories are below:

"Neighborhood Watch"

For the second day in a row our friend in Monrovia was woken up in the middle of the night by calls for help from his neighbors. Two nights ago his neighbor's home was invaded by a robber wielding a cutlass (machete) in the early morning hours. One of the family members was able to text for help in the confusion and quickly word spread to all the neighbors. Within minutes a group of friends stormed the house, grabbed the robber, and dragged him into the streets where the angry mob began to beat him. Eventually the police arrived and were disappointed that the robber was still alive. The robber was beaten nearly to death, but was happy to get away from the mob and get to the safety of the jail.

Last night, around 2 am, another call went out to friends and neighbors for a house fire. As soon as they got the call, everyone grabbed their buckets or large containers of water and ran to the neighbor in need. Even with the help of the fire brigade they couldn't save the mud hut and the fire spread to several other huts, which also burned to the ground. Right after the fire brigade extinguished the last of the smoldering rubble, the torrential rains began again. The fire was caused by the mother who left a lit candle in a bedroom when she went outside to talk to a friend. Luckily no one was hurt.

"Smell, No Taste"

A small town in a rubber forest has a local name I couldn't pronounce (like most villages with local names). Loosely translated, the town is called "smell, no taste." During the war the relatively well supplied peacekeeping troops would cook their food over open fires while the rubber farmers hiding among the trees could smell it, but had nothing to eat for themselves.

"Marriage Problems"

My Liberian friend was telling me about his problems with his wife. He started by stating he didn't think he could be a polygamist, like many Africans, because dealing with one wife was hard enough. After he had been married for four years or so he felt his wife didn't love him and he wanted to get rid of her, so he got another girl pregnant. Eleven years later he has the daughter from the other girl, and the same wife. She stuck by him even though the mother of his child gave him the child and walked away and he adopted another kid from the neighborhood. The kids live with his parents (their grandmother), but he and his wife still share a house in the city. Both work, but both are on the road all the time. When he is at home, she kicks him out and sends him to the club or has his friends pick him up and take him away. What she does at home he doesn't know.

Accra, Ghana. 24 September 2010.

On our way to the airport this morning we stopped to get some snacks at a local market in Monrovia. The store had decent variety of items imported from Europe and South Africa and the first Gatorade I had seen in Africa for about $3.20 (for a quart size bottle). Surprisingly the traffic was light so we arrived at the airport with plenty of time to spare.

As we had extra time before our flight and our driver had connections to Firestone we decided to take a side trip to visit the Firestone farm and it's commissary. The Firestone commissary was stocked with the largest variety of western foods I had seen so far in Africa. They had boxes of tortilla chips, Kraft Mac and Cheese, A&W root beer, Whatchamacallit candy bars, as well as all the western brands of shampoo, deodorant, and personal products. Unfortunately I didn't have room in my suitcase for a case of tortilla chips, which are impossible to find in Dakar.

Brad split from our traveling party at the airport but Natasha and I continued on to Ghana for the second leg of our western Africa trip. We made it to Accra without any issues, rented a car, and were off exploring the city within a couple hours of arrival. Our first stop was the University of Ghana, which has a beautiful campus set on a hill across the valley from the government headquarters. The campus is huge with lots of large buildings, a medical school, law school, large sports fields, and blocks of dorms. We got to stop and watch part of a women's soccer game along with a couple hundred spectators (the light blue team was doing pretty well).

After the tour of the university the rain started to come down again and it started to get dark so we set out to find a place for dinner. We settled on a bamboo-cabana motif restaurant that specialized in local foods. I devoured a local dish of beans and beef called "Red Red" while Natasha enjoyed some fried plantains.

Accra, Ghana. 25 September 2010.

We spent the day on another driving tour of the city and getting ready for the Accra Marathon on Sunday. We found the U.S. Embassy, the Kofi Annan Peacekeeping Center, W.E. DuBois center, the LDS temple, and then spent a couple hours trying to find the shuttle pickup point for the marathon and the marathon headquarters. We finally found the office in a very poorly marked room on the third floor of a building in a back alley, away from the main street.

I decided to take it easy that afternoon and ended up taking a nap before going to a pre-marathon pasta party with a bunch of resident expats. A group of about twenty women were excited to run the 1/2 marathon the following day (husbands were going to watch the kids while the wives ran) and only one other guy was going to run the marathon with me. "Mad Dog" was a 72-year-old American from Florida who had run 335 previous marathons in 105 different countries (he also holds the world record for the person who has run marathons in the most number of countries).

The Accra International Marathon director was also at the dinner and was exhausted from her preparations for the race. I had spoken to her earlier at her office when I was looking for directions to the marathon shuttle and her office was packed with people conducting last minute coordination for the big race. To add to her agony, several local runners had showed up the day before the race to demand a refund of their race registration fee so they could run in the Milo Marathon recently scheduled for the day before the Accra International Marathon. According to her, Milo announced their decision to move their marathon to 25 September on the first of September while her marathon had been scheduled for several months. They also quintupled their prize money for their race (and dwarfing the prize money offered by the Accra International Marathon) so she felt obliged to let the athletes compete for the bigger payday. We had seen the Milo branded buses following driving around town earlier in the day and their awards ceremony on TV where they had claimed over 5000 participants.

Accra, Ghana. 26 September 2010.

Race day! I got up at 3:30 in the morning to carpool with the Accra expats to the marathon shuttle start point at the Salvation Army hostel. At the hostel I linked up with several Peace Corps volunteers who had assembled from the neighboring countries to run the marathon. The shuttle bus arrived an hour late (scheduled for 4:30) and after a tumultuous hour long ride through the city dropped off the 1/2 marathoners at their start point and then continued another 13.1 miles to our start point- a dashed line spray painted across the road in the middle of nowhere. As there were no porta-potties at the start point and only small bushes in the vicinity, many white rear ends were visible in the grass as people used the bathroom before the start of the race.

A few of the brave Africans who had run the Milo Marathon the day before lined up again at the start line, some boasting about their accomplishments the day before and bragging they were going to win today (mostly exaggerations in my opinion- one guy claimed to have run a 2:10 marathon the day before). About 50 of us toed the starting line, including 20 Africans, and after four false starts, because the starting pistol kept misfiring, we were off, over an hour after the scheduled start (actual start at 6:45).

The Africans were off like a shot out of a pistol and quickly out of sight while the westerners started plodding down the road. A couple other runners like me wore hydration backpacks as the marathon had received terrible reviews last year for not having enough aid stations and running out of water halfway through the race. I was happy to find many aid stations along the course and even at some spots a case of water dropped so you could help yourself. However in some of the more congested locations I think the locals may have walked away with the water.

There was a light cooling mist as we ran through the hills in the first half of the marathon and I reached the midway point in just over two hours (2:02). I grabbed a couple bottles and refilled my 2-liter hydration pack and started to alternate short walks with my running. The sun came out and the weather quickly became hot and humid. By mile 16 I was dehydrated and getting sore. My walks got longer and my running shorter and within a couple miles my stride was significantly shortened.

I was already regretting my decision to run the full marathon as my longest training run in preparation for the marathon was only 14.25 miles and the heat in Dakar had forced me to walk at the end of that run too. My buddy, Brad, had talked me into running the full marathon with him, but then an emergency came up at home so he had to skip the Ghana leg, and the Accra Marathon, part of the trip. So I had to run the distance alone… As I passed the torturous miles alone in agony I contemplated revenge.

Around mile 20 we ran up a hill into a village and passed people coming home from church dressed in their Sunday best. Many churches were still in session and played a variety of music- some just singing loud into their speakers, others accompanied by trumpets, while others featured full rock bands, seemingly in competition to be the loudest or heard above the rest. Some of the locals yelled encouragement to my shuffling steps, yelling "fast, fast!" Others just read my face and told me the truth: "you look tired."

A couple miles later we emerged from the village onto the main commercial street that lead into Accra and had to weave our way through traffic. The sidewalks were full of vendors and walkers. The side of the road had buses and taxis zooming in to stop and pick up passengers, and heavy traffic dominated the main lanes so making forward progress became a lot more difficult. Sometimes I had to stop and wait for traffic or people to move aside so I could try to stumble forward, but with only three miles to go I had hope.

We finally got clear of the market and the thick foot traffic with two miles to go so I decided to do my best to run the rest of the way in and finish strong. I figured it was only two miles to go, and I had run that distance many times before, so it should be easy. I made it one mile running at a decent pace before I fell apart. I couldn't lift my legs anymore and walking even hurt so bad I wanted to stop and lie down in the dirt on the side of the road.

At that point of desperation the race director pulled up in her car and handed me a bottle of water and cheered me to keep going. I kept going forward. I had to grit my teeth and limp along as my left leg froze up and wouldn't bend anymore and my right foot felt so bruised and I could only step with my heel. It took me 25 minutes to walk that last mile and it felt like it was going to last forever under the scorching sun.

Finally I reached some large banners flying on the side of the road and a cut through some high grass that led to the finish line. I managed to shuffle and almost broke into tears as I crossed the finish line, five hours and sixteen minutes after I began.

My first priority was water and I wasn't the only one suffering. The girl that finished after me collapsed at the finish line and had to be carried to the first aid tent (I felt a little envious). Others were lying in the shade and medics were walking around pouring water on people or rubbing them with ice. The race director even collapsed and was helped into the shade and given ice.

A couple liters of water later I was feeling better and an hour or so later lunch was served. It seemed like a riot was going to break out when they started to run out of food, but eventually I got my plate of chicken and rice. It was pretty good and I quickly wolfed it down local style using my hands as no forks were provided. Later on they handed out goodie bags and finally the race medal! I then retreated to my hotel and ended up sleeping six hours before dinner and heading to bed again.

People in the hotel kept staring at me as I limped around, and didn't seem to believe that I had just ran a marathon.

Accra, Ghana. 27 September 2010.
The day after the Accra Marathon Natasha and I set off to explore

more of Ghana. Even though we left before 7am, it still took an hour to get out of Accra thanks to persistent traffic in the city. Three hours later we made it to Cape Coast and the huge fortress that was the point of no return for hundreds of thousands of Africans shipped out as slaves. The Cape Coast Castle is now a museum and popular tourist destination for millions of visitors despite its terrible history.

We started by visiting the museum and its collection of artifacts from Ghana's past. They have a detailed display that explains many aspects of the culture and daily life for Ghanaians. There is also a larger section dedicated to the slave trade and how Africans and Europeans were enriched through the trade triangle. I thought it was interesting that some Christian church leaders in that time period advocated the importation of African slaves to the Americas as the Native Americans were too weak and dying from European diseases. The African slaves were recognized as much stronger, healthier, and disease resistant and therefore a better source of labor. The Europeans gave weapons freely to the local African leaders to help them in their tribal wars and then accepted the prisoners of war the Africans captured as slaves.

The most significant part of the tour to me was the visit to the dungeons or slave holding areas where they slaves were usually held for a minimum of four months while they were waiting to be loaded onto the westward bound ships. Upwards of a thousand slaves could be held at a time with almost no light and a narrow channel gouged into the stone floor for the human waste to evacuate down the large chamber into the sea. Unruly slaves were packed in a smaller chamber that measured about 20ft by 10ft, but held up to 200 at a time. When the building was being renovated several years ago, excavators had to dig through two feet of human waste to reach the stone floor underneath. A tunnel at the end of the large holding chamber where the main populations of the slaves were held led to the door of no return and the ships waiting offshore. Now a monument to represent the end of the slave trade blocks that tunnel. The rest of the tour focuses on the white living quarters and the church above the dungeons and was boring compared to the slave dungeons.

After lunch, we drove out to Kakum National Park, a tropical rain forest that features a quarter-mile canopy walk, a narrow rope bridge suspended 120ft above the ground. The bridge is hung in a circular route consisting of eight segments tied to huge trees. 12-inch wide planks form the walking surface and every movement and breeze made the bridge swing. It was a pretty cool view, but we couldn't see any animals or the ground through the layers of thick trees.

After sliding down the hill from the tree top platforms and walkways we drove two more hours back to Accra in order to fight another two hours of traffic to get back to our hotel.

Accra, Ghana. 28 September 2010.

On my last day in Ghana we visited the monument and museum for first President of Ghana, Dr. Kwame Nkrumah. It's a nice park with an outdoor display of the many books he wrote, lots of trees planted by visiting dignitaries, and a huge pyramid-like monument surrounded by a large reflecting pond and many statues. The display tells the story of Dr. Kwame Nkrumah and has many pictures of where he grew up, his influences, and his memorable quotes. Inside the monument is his tomb. Behind the monument is a museum with more pictures and artifacts from the life of the first president of Ghana. Exhibits include all his old dorm furniture from when he was an undergrad student at Lincoln University in Pennsylvania.

I was also able to visit the Kofi Anan International Peacekeeping Center, which was located near the end of the Accra Marathon, a location I was so glad to see a couple days ago. The Kofi center was part of three regional peacekeeping centers in West Africa designed to assist in the development of the African Standby Force. Each regional training center was sponsored by a different foreign military and the Kofi center was sponsored by the US military and a US Marine Corps Colonel gave us a brief tour of the center. He explained that the Kofi center focused on the operational level of military planning and operations and the French sponsored center in Bamako, Mali trained at the tactical level, and the third center in Nigeria was sponsored by the British and focused on the strategic level.

The Koffi Center facilities were nice with a large gym, dorm rooms for participants and modern classrooms with wifi and computers. We walked into one class where a couple of American soldiers were teaching a class on deploying units and equipment by air, ground, and sea to a fictional battlefield in Africa. Our Marine guide explained that this wasn't just a US effort but the center received funding from different countries that also provided instructors. The center offered a number of courses that all African and many international military students could attend throughout the year.

Ghana Stories

"Girl hairstyles in Ghana"

Almost all the young girls or school age girls keep their hair very short (like the boys) while they are in school. Our guide in explaining the tradition related that the headmaster at his daughter's school requires all girls to keep their hair very short, almost shaved. When they get married, the women traditionally start wearing headscarves to cover their hair.

"Self-guided Sheep & Goats"

On the outskirts of town and in the villages herds of goats and sheep are seen walking around, crossing the roads, and generally walking with a purpose. However, usually they have no human or animal supervision. The goats are trained to follow a certain route and take themselves out to pasture and come back to the house later on, all automatically and without supervision.

"Cell Service Carrier Advertising"

In Ghana the competition between cell phone service providers is heating up and advertising has become a major competition between the different brands. All the major brands advertise: MTN, Vodafone, Tigo, Zain; but it seems the most intense battle is between Vodafone and MTN. Their battle has spread from the airwaves to the fabric of people's clothes (incorporating both small and large logos), as well as the color of their house and business. Walking down the street in some areas it seems that the houses alternate red (Vodafone) and yellow (MTN).

"Garbage Man Jingle"

Around 5am one morning I was woken by the sound of what I thought was the ice-cream man driving through the streets of Accra. It was a meandering thin tune played endlessly over speaker, just like an ice-cream man who sells from a truck common in North America. The reality couldn't be more opposite, because this tune in Accra announced the coming of the garbage man, and people would rush to bring their garbage out.

"Days of the Week Names"

I noticed that many Ghanians shared the same name and I was told they were often named for the day of the week that they were born. For boys; Monday was Kwoajo, Tuesday was Kwabewa, Wednesday was Kwaku, Thursday was Yako, Friday was Koffi, Saturday was Kwame, and Sunday was Kwesi. For girls the names for the same days were Adoja, Abena, Akya, Yaa, Afia, Awa, and Akosua. If I had been born in Ghana my name would have been Kwaku.

4 SENEGAL TRAVELS

Dakar, Senegal. 4 October 2010.

I was invited by a friend who worked at the African Center for Strategic Studies in Dakar to attend a special conference on the integration and training of females in the Senegalese military and I couldn't say no to this interesting topic. Many African militaries reflect their paternalistic societies where women usually only play an extremely limited supporting role on the side lines and this American initiative to support women in the military would be interesting.

The Senegalese Minister of State and the Deputy Chief of Mission from the U.S. Embassy opened the conference and the room was full of Senegalese female officers (I counted over 200 people in the packed room with people standing in the aisles and along the walls). The guest speaker was U.S. Marine Corps Major General Garrett, the highest ranking female officer in the Marines and she spoke to issues common in both the US and Senegalese militaries. She then fielded questions from the audience about women in combat, maternity leave, having kids and a military career.

The most challenging question was to the dual roles of female officers as being both a leader at work and being a worker at home, subservient to the husband. I imagine this could be difficult for American female officers as well but probably not to the same extent as to some countries in Africa where the wives expect to be beaten by their husbands.

Dakar, Senegal. 6 October 2010.

In my travels in Senegal and elsewhere in Africa the locals had constantly asked me on how to get a visa to the United States. On one occasion I even had a customs officer in the Dakar airport ask me for help with his visa so I talked to a friend who worked at the American embassy about how the visa system works. She invited me into the embassy to watch some visa interviews and explained the process to me.

The visa process for the U.S. was a multistep process where the applicants first filled out their application online, gathered the required documents (passport, photos, forms, fees), and went to the embassy on a day when they conducted interviews. In Dakar the consular section didn't conduct interviews everyday but posted a schedule and usually a line formed early in the morning (larger embassies had different schedules). The documents would then be evaluated and if everything was in order the person would be interviewed by a consular officer who would ask questions about why they wanted to go to the U.S., what they were going to do, how would they support themselves, and how they were going to get back.

Roughly 50% of all the applicants were refused because they didn't have a plan and it appeared that they were going to the U.S. without intent to return. The consular officer said there were immigration programs available from time to time such as the diversity visa but the only interviews I was able to observe were for tourist visas. It was clear to me that many had no plan to come home but many others had legitimate cases such as going to college or Disneyland. Most of the visas granted were business related to participate in conferences, buy cars for import to Senegal, or to purchase other products and bring them back. Specific items included hair extensions, cosmetics, clothes, electronics, and even construction equipment- all items that are limited and expensive in the local markets.

The Diversity Visa offered the best chance for the average Senegalese to immigrate to the U.S. but it was a long process. It took 18 months for the lucky candidate to progress from the application to the final interview and the Dakar office was responsible for processing applications from four additional countries in the region. The main requirements were to be from an under-represented country in the U.S. and have a high school diploma or worked in a skilled job for at least two years. If the visa was granted the immigrant could take their spouse and kids with them, but this was also where fraud often appeared as someone could pay to become a spouse for immigration purposes. Visa fraud was a concern but the consular officer was happy to help people visit or immigrate for the right reasons.

Dakar, Senegal. 15 October 2010.

One of my duties at the Embassy in Dakar is to conduct the English language testing for Senegalese military who are applying to attend military training in the U.S. As training given in the states is provided only in English, the Senegalese applicants would need to be proficient in English. The U.S. government therefore provided two English language labs in Dakar where Senegalese troops can study English and attend English language courses taught by American trained English teachers.

My job was to go to the language labs monthly to administer the English test, grade the tests, and report the scores back to the embassy. The test was fairly simple with a listening and a reading portion with a test booklet. For the test we would use the headphones and cassette player to play the listening portion and the applicant would fill in their responses by filling in the corresponding answer bubble on a scantron answer sheet. Often explaining how to fill out the answer sheet was the biggest challenge in administering the test, as many Africans are unfamiliar with standardized testing with computer-graded exams.

The test would take about two hours to administer with reading the instructions in English, translating them into French, often someone else then translating the instructions again into Wolof or some other local dialect. Then often there was the challenge of the test takers not having glasses and having to send a runner out to borrow glasses from someone else. Then once the tests had all been counted and accounted for I would grade the tests by hand as I didn't have a scantron reader myself.

In general, an applicant would need to score 55 out of 100 points (100 questions on the exam) in order to qualify to go to training in the United States. The more complex classes such as at the War College required much higher scores in the 90s. If an applicant was otherwise well qualified and missed the required score by less than ten points we could arrange a waiver and send them to English training in the states before attending the actual course. For this test, the high score was a 92 (by an enlisted artilleryman) followed by 85, 81, 76, 73, 63, 60, 60, 59, 52, 46, and 44.

Attending U.S. military training in the United States was like hitting the jackpot because not only would the traveler fly to the U.S., they would stay in American barracks, eat in the American dining facility, get a boost in their pay, be able to shop at American stores, as well as go on cultural tours. Upon return they would then be considered experts in their new skills, usually be promoted, and placed in an instructor roll where they could share their expertise with others. We often saw Senegalese and other African troops proudly wearing their badges earned at American military schools.

Dakar, Senegal. 26 October 2010.

It pays to have friends at the Embassy. Dakar is considered by many to be the Paris of West Africa and many diplomatic missions to the region are based in Dakar. It's a common game to guess what national flag is above a building because there are so many embassies here. A friend invited me to attend the Austrian National Day celebration at the Austrian Chief of Mission residence (Ambassador's house) and I got to dress up and hang out by the pool in a nice mansion near the beach.

The food was amazing and it was by far the best I had eaten in weeks with mini sandwiches, brochettes (Kabobs), and all kinds of small items as well as an open bar. I met a number of local businessmen who were selling well drilling equipment, construction equipment, bottled water, as well as representatives from various NGOs. A live band played throughout the evening and I was surprised to meet the Ambassador from Zimbabwe in the receiving line. She was a nice little old white lady who was excited to hear that I had just run in the Victoria Falls 1/2 Marathon.

Dakar, Senegal. 28 October 2010.

Most of October was spent in Dakar, researching trips in the morning and surfing in the afternoon, but finally I was able to get on the road again. I had five friends fly in from Europe, Mozambique, and Ethiopia for a week to cruise around Senegal. The first couple days I took them around Dakar to the usual sites- Goree Island, African Renaissance Monument, Place de l'independance, N'Gor island, and even a boat SCUBA dive off N'Gor Island. Now we are driving inland and touring Thies and a couple other cities to give them a taste of the real Senegal.

The drive from Dakar thru Rufisque was surprisingly easy today but scared my European friends. We made the 70km drive in an amazing

90 minutes given our 11am start time. In Thies they kept remarking about how many westerners were wandering around. My female African-American friend kept getting hit on by Senegalese men and even got a marriage proposal while we were waiting for lunch. Overall it was a good day despite my friends broken Frenglish and temps soaring above 41*C/106*F. The next day we are going further inland in search of a city described as the dirtiest, filthiest, downright worst city in Senegal to see if it lives up to it's reputation. It should be fun!

Touba, Senegal. 29 October 2010.

This morning we woke up in Thies and drove down to the dirtiest, nastiest place in Senegal. Kaolack had a nice mosque but the town was flooded with many buildings knee to hip deep in green water and a meter-wide stream of foul murky water ran along the side of the road. Huge piles of garbage rotted everywhere you looked and it's ripe smell filled the air. Goats, cows, and people waded through the muck and cars and scooters were mired in traffic.

Somehow I found an oasis on the edge of town, a little resort on the river that was clean and didn't stink, where we ate lunch. As we left two busloads of white tourists pulled up to the hotel to discharge their unfortunate passengers. If Kaolack was their final destination in Senegal they were in for an disappointing vacation.

From Kaolack we drove three hours north to the sacred city of Touba and met the spiritual leader of the Mouride Muslims. Upon arrival in the sandy city we were ushered into his large chamber where he greets his visitors and supplicants, a large room 20'x40', and lined with couches and deep plush carpets. For the next half hour we discussed Islam and his education initiatives in Touba and the construction of a new university on the outskirts of town.

After our meeting with the esteemed spiritual guide we met and dined with the president of an Islamic education program in Touba. We discussed the school he had developed that took Islamic education and added Senegalese culture programs as well as secular scientific training to develop a well-rounded, spiritual Muslim.

After dinner we returned to my friend's house in Touba where we spent the night. Their great grandfather had founded Touba and was enshrined in the grande mosque. His image is everywhere in Senegal-the image of a man in a white turban with a part of turban covering his mouth. My friends spent the night telling us stories about their great grandfather and his many accomplishments. He sounded like a fascinating person who went through many trials and was a great spiritual leader for Senegal. According to the stories he was thrown into the lion's den but emerged unharmed after two days, he was put into a furnace but did not burn, and was exiled for many years. In the end he returned victorious to Senegal, wrote many books, taught many people, and preserved the Senegalese culture.

Touba, Senegal. 30 October 2010.

My friends and I spent the day wandering around the hot sandy streets of Touba barefoot. We started the day with a late breakfast with our host followed by a tour of the Grande Mosque. The building is very impressive and I have never been inside a building so elaborate or ornate.

The Grande Mosque took decades to be built and is continually being added onto and expanded. Across the street we visited the library and saw many of the books written by Cheikh Amadou Bamba and learned more of his story. Our guide said that he wrote over 7.5 tons of books and all of it could not be read in a lifetime.

As soon as we left the mosque people begging for money, both young and old, mobbed us. So many kids surrounded our vehicles and were tapping our windows that some started to climb onto the roof rack to try to get our attention. We had to cut our visit short so no one would get hurt.

We drove north through a couple hundred potholed kilometers of the Senegalese countryside to reach Saint Louis at the North Western corner of the country. We passed millions of goats and cows and a couple camel herds in the peanut fields in the middle of the Sahel. Saint Louis was a nice change of pace and we wandered out to the fishing village and ate dinner overlooking the river as the sun set.

Saint Louis, Senegal. 31 October 2010.

Saint Louis was nice and relaxing, more calm than usual since it was a Sunday morning. We toured the museum at the southern end of the island as well as the art museum by the Hotel Sidone. Our plan was to drive back on the coastal beach to Dakar but the tide was too high to make the passage as in some places the thick jungle spilled into the ocean at high tide.

We ended up driving down the road to Kebemer and then to Tiougoune on the coast. There was a nice fishing village at the end of the road with a new fish processing area where the locals could clean and dry their catch in the sun. Our goal was to try to drive down the coast from Kebemer by the Sea but still the tide was too high and we couldn't make the drive on the beach. Eventually we made it back to Thies where we ate lunch and then to home in Dakar.

Dakar, Senegal. 1 November 2010.

Senegal is a great place for holidays! Senegal celebrates all Muslim and Catholic holidays so today Dakar was still a ghost town and we could move around easily as traffic was light. In the morning we drove out to Lac Rose, a small saltwater lake north of Dakar that was made famous as the former finish line of the Paris-Dakar rally and its pink waters. The lake turns pink in the dry season in certain light, but today the water looked golden to me. Dozens of locals were in the water scooping salt water off the bottom of the lake and bringing it ashore in boats where it was piled in large heaps on the beach.

As soon as we stepped out of the car the local vendors selling all kinds of trinkets swarmed us. Today the big items being offered to us were sand paintings and cups made from cow horns. Since the vendors were so aggressive we didn't stay too long by the salt piles and we ended up driving around most of the lake.

After a quick lunch at a nearby restaurant we went diving again off N'Gor Island and saw several schools of hand-sized fish, a couple Morey eels, and other larger fish. I was the first one to run out of air on the dive and had to share with the dive master to stay under with the group. Everyone says the best way to increase my bottom time is to dive more often so I'll have to keep at it. We ended up with 32 minutes of bottom time at 26 meters.

Later we took the pirogue out to N'Gor Island to tour the top side of the island and watched the surfers on the west side. The waves were waist high and bigger and five or six surfers had taken the boat from N'Gor beach and were getting some decent rides. We ate dinner at sunset on the water then took the pirogue back to the beach in the dark.

5 NIGERIA & GUINEA-BISSAU

Lagos, Nigeria. 6 November 2010.

Traffic sucks in Lagos, but besides that it is an interesting city where super yachts costing millions share the muddy waters with swamped pirogues. Oil is king in Nigeria and contributes more than $7 billion every year to the government of Nigeria but it's hard to see where it benefits regular Nigerians on the street. Nobody is sure of the exact population of Lagos or Nigeria, but there are an estimated 20 million in Lagos and over 110 million in Nigeria. If the estimates are correct then approximately 1 of every 5 Africans is Nigerian and within twenty years 1 out of 3 Africans will be Nigerian.

Natasha, myself, and another group of friends met up in Nigeria for a tour of the country, however, due to security concerns we were restricted to Lagos for our week in Nigeria. In Lagos it seemed that the walls of the residential compounds were a meter higher than Dakar and many of the newer cars we saw in the city were light armored vehicles. Truckloads of soldiers were stationed at every major intersection and we frequently saw military vehicles on the street.

There are a lot of nice places in Lagos, as yesterday I ate lunch at Kentucky Fried Chicken and it was pretty good, just like I remembered from the last time I ate KFC in the states. We visited a couple modern shopping malls where I found a few well stocked bookstores and bought "Allah is not Obliged" and "Half of a Yellow Sun," both by Nigerian authors and highly recommended.

We also visited the Lekki Market and I bought two impressionistic paintings depicting buses stuck in traffic, a typical scene in Lagos. The market was like any other artisan market targeting tourists that I have seen in Africa. Some kids helped us find a parking spot, then tried to push us into their favorite shops, which all sold the same stuff. Popular items were wooden monkeys (hear, speak, see no evil with a 4th pregnant monkey), ivory tusks, cheetah and leopard skins, and local paintings. As soon as I bought my paintings another kid showed up and grabbed my stuff to serve as my porter and followed me around the market. I ended up buying the kid a fortified milk drink when I stopped to buy a bottle of water. His handler was upset when he saw my porter with his drink because he thought the porter was drinking his profits. A pickpocket tried to lift my colleague's wallet but was blocked by my colleague putting his hands into his pockets. Someone else walked by and bumped my rear pockets to see if I had anything back there while I had my hands in my front pockets. My porter snickered but denied any knowledge of the pickpocket when we asked him about it.

As we returned to the vehicle to drive back to the hotel we were swarmed by kids again asking for several thousand Naira for school supplies as well as crippled kids asking for handouts. Then the parking attendant kid had his hand out again even though he was already paid. When the older kids saw us paying the porters they came over to make sure they got their cut too and the porters had to give up their money.

Overall, the beggars and hawkers in Lagos are on par with Senegal. However, since we were staying in a luxury hotel in a nice neighborhood in Lagos the beggar/hawker population was limited.

Vehicles bristling with police machine guns frequently passed on the streets and security guards armed with Kalashnikovs were positioned on the perimeter of hotels and buildings. The walls seemed to be at least three feet higher here and were frequently topped with razor wire and sharpened spikes. There was also usually some kind of armored or SWAT vehicle at the major intersections and cameras were everywhere important.

Lagos, Nigeria. 8 November 2010.

I made some friends at Shell and Chevron and spent the last couple days hanging out in their respective compounds. On the oil compounds it's like living back in Europe or the States complete with lush green softball fields, people grilling outside, and little kids riding skateboards and bikes on the smooth paved roads. One hundred meters away taxis and motorcycles fly down bumpy dirt roads in the chaos of Nigerian traffic, dodging broken down buses, and ditches filled with muddy waste. The difference is like night and day when you get away from the expensive hotels and shopping malls and see how the majority of people live in Lagos.

Oil is where it's at and it is a different world in Nigeria if you have money. The International School costs about $20,000 USD per kid each year, but if you work for an oil company the company covers the cost. For the adults there are many adult establishments that offer "local content" or an opportunity to experience local culture. A friend went to a club called "Ynot" and described it as every teenage boys fantasy: more than 150 of the most beautiful women you had ever seen all excited to see you and insisting on spending the evening with you. He said the beer and alcohol flowed freely but he had to fight to leave before things got too serious with his dates for the night. Three huge bouncers accompanied him to his cab and made sure he was safe while he waited, a contrast to the recent past where robberies were common outside the clubs.

Lagos, Nigeria. 9 November 2010.

All in all the trip to Lagos was not that exciting as our ability to get out and explore the city and surrounding area was extremely limited due to security concerns. In the end we ended up mostly hanging out at the pool at the hotel or in the hotel restaurants. The majority of the hotels clients were wealthy and we met the notable American politician, Jessie Jackson, in the hotel lobby. I was relieved when our week in Lagos was up and I was able to return to Senegal. The rest of the group also split up and headed back to their respective homes.

Dakar, Senegal. 10-14 November 2010.

Military and civilian leaders from the 15 member states of ECOWAS met in Dakar for a week-long conference to discuss regional challenges, the makeup and mission of the ECOWAS Battalion, and deeper theoretical questions such as what is the role of the Army in a nation, what should be the ethnic composition of an Army, should the Army have a political role? Most of the delegations presented a topic and all engaged in the discussion via simultaneous translation as the delegates spoke combinations of French, Portuguese and English.

One of the more interesting discussions was on the gradient of roles between the Army and the Police in regards to border security, internal stability, and public order. How gendarmes interface with the Army and Police was an interesting wrinkle as well, especially in regard to less governed spaces and territorial integrity. Other roles, such as disaster response, were given to the Army.

Dakar, Senegal. 14 November 2010.

I have always wanted to learn to sail and today I had my first lesson, and my first wreck at the Dakar Yacht Club. The good news is that nobody got hurt and the boat wasn't damaged. The bad news was that we couldn't self-recover and we spent about 30 minutes in the water waiting for the motorboat to come out and help recover the boat. Everybody told me when we got back to the shore that the Hobie Cat was designed to flip over, self recover, then keep on sailing but even with the help of the instructor and another person we couldn't get the boat to right itself without the motorboat.

Sailing was pretty cool, especially when we started to pick up some speed. The instructor kept telling me that we weren't supposed to take any risks today, but I still managed to flip the boat. I can't wait until I can run one by myself, hike out on the trapeze, and then probably flip the boat again.

Bissau, Guinea-Bissau. 15-17 November 2010.

Three days is not enough time to see all of Guinea-Bissau. Due to transportation constraints we were stuck in Bissau for the entire trip and missed out on visiting the Archipelago World Heritage Sites-hopefully I will have the opportunity to come back!

I visited Bissau with a US Coast Guard Port Assessment team in order to translate for the team as I was one of the few Americans at the US Embassy that could speak Portuguese. Our first stop in Bissau we met with the government leaders from the Secretary of State for Transportation and Communications where we discussed high-level trade and transportation agreements between the US and Guinea-Bissau. Guinea-Bissau had just received $20million from the World Bank for improvements to the port and was focusing on developing the infrastructure that would increase revenue. Security and interdiction of prohibited items were also key concerns of the group as many illicit things are trafficked through West Africa such as drugs and weapons.

I was surprised to learn that the main exports of the port were cashews (to Portugal), "ferro velho" or scrap metal (to India) and other fruits (to Cape Verde). There was a company dredging the port and pulling up sunken metal ships, chopping them up, and shipping them out in containers as scrap metal. This was an essential mission as many of the boat slips were blocked by partially submerged boats, which in turn limited port capacity.

We also met with the Secretary of Defense and discussed security of the port and the surrounding waters. The Secretary asked for US assistance in strengthening their military and was curious as to why the US was concerned about illegal fishing in their territorial waters. He stated that fishing was an important food source for the country. The Secretary continued that since the war they only had boats that were capable of patrolling rivers and lacked the capacity to go out into the open seas to interdict illegal fishing boats or traffickers.

Our port assessment team then visited the Port Security Office and met their European-trained team and toured the port. The port in Bissau offered no ship services (food, water, and repairs) and saw limited traffic, mostly from Cape Verde. The Port Police secured the port and inspected ships and containers and controlled both the port and the adjacent container yard. The container yard was interesting as the containers were stacked in a dirt lot between the port and the main road. Large wheeled forklifts stacked containers three or four high in rows along the road or shoreline

We next met with the Deputy Police Commissioner who explained how they interfaced and interacted with the Port Police and military. The Police force also had a special maritime police that was different than the Coast Guard. During the visit we met with the Maritime Police, the Port Police, Frontier Guard, the National Guard, Regular Police, Army, Navy, and the Coast Guard. There was also a Customs Police, Forestry Police, and Immigration Police that we did not meet.

The Deputy Police Commissioner made an interesting statement that not that long ago there weren't any drugs in the region. They first found illegal drugs in 2004 when some Columbians dropped bags from an airplane into the sea. Some local fisherman found the bags and thought they contained fertilizer and put it on their crops, killing them. They didn't realize the substance had any value. Since then the police developed a narco-trafficking unit under the Ministry of Interior and had taken action such as closing the border on the road leading to Conakry. The police asserted that the drugs were never consumed in Bissau, just transited to other locations.

I loved my short time in Bissau- I was able to speak Portuguese again, drank Guarana every day, and everything reminded me of living in the country outside of Rio de Janeiro, especially the red dirt. Even the toilets in the hotel had signs posted to remind users to not flush the toilet paper.

I went for a couple early morning runs during my visit to Bissau and saw several remarkable sights: the former Presidential Palace which was destroyed in the war, the markets alongside the road mostly selling shoes and food, the new National Assembly building recently built by the Chinese, and so on. All the little kids were excited to see me run by; I was a novelty, like they hadn't seen many Toubabs, especially not running through their neighborhoods in the early morning hours.

Along the side of the road young men would wait with wheelbarrows for an opportunity to unload and carry stuff. During my last run a pickup truck pulled up to a group of guys with wheelbarrows and started to offload the carcasses of several butchered cows, which were then wheeled off down the dirt back alleys to some restaurants or smaller butcher stands.

The majority of the cars on the road were taxis, older Mercedes D190s painted blue and white. These tough old cars are desperately needed because the roads in Bissau are in very poor shape. Most of the people traveled by foot or blue and yellow vans. There were a couple modern gas stations in town, but on the outskirts of town fuel was sold by the bottle or jug. I think that most of the fuel was for generator use as the town did not provide electricity for the use for the average person. If you wanted power you had to buy a generator and few people could afford one or the fuel required. Light after dark is a luxury in Guinea-Bissau.

Only the street vendors were eager to talk to me. The day before Tabaski they claimed they needed to make a sale because of the coming holiday, but nobody knew the name of the holiday. The next day about half of them were out selling again on the holiday. The vendors said they rarely saw any foreigners anymore and business was very slow. The rest of the people I saw just kind of watched me walk or run by but didn't stare too long.

Leaving Bissau was interesting as well. The airport doesn't have any computers so they kept the passenger's electronic tickets and wrote out a roster of all the passengers. When we made it to the security checkpoint we were wanded, groped, and then passed through a metal detector that wasn't plugged in. The bag scanner wasn't plugged in either and a couple people at a desk behind it hand searched your bag. Since it was Tabaski they also had a donation sheet so you could give them money to help them celebrate. When I asked what they were going to buy, one young lady responded "Bebidas" or alcohol and made the universal gesture for drinking.

The pilot stuck his head into the terminal 45 minutes before the scheduled departure and counted people sitting in the lobby. Since we were all there he told us to load the plane and we took off early and got to Dakar in an hour (flight was scheduled to take 1 hour and 35 minutes).

Dakar, Senegal. 25 November 2010.

I finally got my paintings from Nigeria framed for 5,000 CFA each (about $10 each). These frames should last for a long time as there is a 1/4" plywood sheet nailed to the back of each one and an industrial strength metal eyelet screwed in the top for hanging.

I also ventured into the Sandaga Outdoor Market again yesterday on a special mission: to purchase a Baye Fall boubou made of long strips of fabric. As usual when I entered the market someone approached me and asked if I wanted to see his artisan store selling all kinds of special items that he made by himself. My new friend led me through the back alleys to the same five-story shirt factory near the north edge of the market. Inside he took me to the boubou room and we began our negotiations. Since I was almost a local now he said he would give me a better price than the tourist price- only 110,000 CFA per boubou instead of the ClubMed price of 220,000 CFA each. I countered for 5,000 CFA. We went back and forth over the price for the next half hour and they brought out other examples of boubous of differing quality. In the end I walked away with 3 boubous for 45,000 CFA or 15,000 CFA each (about $30 each). If I had negotiated harder I should have been able to get them for 10,000 each.

Every time I have entered the Sandaga Market I was picked up by a different person and carefully guided to the shirt factory along routes that did not offer boubous or similar items. Upon arrival each of my friends would offer me a tour of their factory and end up in a room where we would negotiate a price. Upon reaching a price we would go to one of the cashiers, either on the third floor or in the gift shop on the ground floor and my friend would hand them the cash and keep a portion for themselves. Communications with cashier are conducted in Wolof and money is exchanged out of sight so I haven't been able to figure out the actual cost of the items. However, a local friend told me he could get boubous for about 5,000 CFA each.

Tabaski, the Muslim celebration of Abraham's sacrifice of the ram instead of his son, was celebrated last week and was a two-day national holiday. According to a friend of mine who returned to his home village for the celebration, each family should sacrifice a male sheep. If they can't afford a male sheep a female sheep would be an acceptable substitute and a goat could be used as a last resort. He was able to provide one male sheep for his family and bought his sheep for next year as well. My friend said the price of the sheep depends on it's size, but an average size sheep would cost between 150,000 to 200,000 CFA ($300-$400 USD) the week before Tabaski. He bought his slightly smaller sheep for next year for 75,000 CFA ($150 USD) and over the next year his family will try to fatten it up.

The day after the Tabaski celebration I went for a run along the beach and found lots of horns and sheep skins stretched out and drying in the sun. A surfer friend told me that he went for a surf after Tabaski and ended up paddling through sheep guts and carcasses because the remains were thrown into the ocean by the locals.

Venice, Italy. 1-12 December 2010.

Half way through my year in Africa all of us Foreign Area Officers in regional training in sub-Saharan Africa were invited to the U.S. Army Africa headquarters in Vicenza, Italy for a conference. The purpose of the conference was to share lessons learned from our trips, discuss applications for graduate school after our time in Africa, and to relax before heading back to Africa for another six months. I was also notified that I was selected for a full-ride scholarship to any graduate school in American that offered a program in international relations and African studies.

Many took the opportunity to visit the American doctors and dentists on the Army base as medical and dental services are lacking on the African continent. Away from the conference, Brad and I rented a car to explore the region. We drove to the Dolomite Mountains and wound our way up the Cliffside roads to the village of Asiago to sample its famous cheese. Later we explored the canals and cathedrals in Venice. It was a good break and welcome change from the heat in Dakar.

Boise, Idaho. 14-31 December 2010.

After two weeks in Venice I flew back to the states to spend Christmas with my family. There was more snow in Italy than in Boise but it was good to spend the holidays with family and friends. During the break I read several books to get ready for my next couple trips. I read Black Man's Burden, Africa in Chaos, Into Africa, China Safari, Escape from Rwanda, Machete Season, A Walk to Remember, I wish to Inform You..., and Dead Aid.

☐

6 ETHIOPIA, DJIBOUTI, & KENYA

Addis Ababa, 9 January 2010.

After passing the holidays in Europe and the states I was glad to finally be back in Africa. It took me 45 hours of traveling to return to Senegal from the west coast of the United States, then another eight hours to get to Addis. I am definitely enjoying the cooler weather in this part of Africa after the long hot fall (and not the freezing cold in the states or Europe).

I flew to Addis on Ethiopian Airlines and I wasn't impressed with the service on Ethiopian or the quality of the aircraft. The service was horrible, the stewardesses ignored my frequent requests for a headset or blanket leaving me cold and watching a needlessly silent movie. The carpet was peeling up around my seat and the poor maintenance of the interior of the plane made me wonder if there were bigger problems elsewhere and if the plane was airworthy!

On the ground in Ethiopia it was a different story. The capital city of Addis Ababa was impressive from the start. The airport was the biggest and nicest I have seen so far in Africa. Roads are great in the city and it's not hard to get around. There was an impressive mix of shiny new tall buildings, grand boulevards and government buildings as well as regal churches and monuments. The people seem nice and I haven't been mobbed by people trying to sell me junk as soon as I get out of the vehicle or exit a building.

I traveled to Ethiopia to meet a group of friends on a visit to several countries in the Horn of Africa region and we all stayed at Natasha's house by the airport. On the first day of our trip we wandered around the city and enjoyed the light Sunday traffic as Natasha drove us around in her SUV. As we travelled down the Ethiopian roadways we discovered that for an English speaking country most of the signs are written in Amharic! Fortunately the important signs, as far as I can tell, are also written in English.

We ate dinner at an Ethiopian cultural restaurant that featured a traditional Ethiopian meal where you ripped off pieces of a flat bread (Njera) and used it to grab the pieces of meat arrayed on a large communal platter with lentils and sauces. While you ate with your hands a traditional four-piece Ethiopian band played songs important to their culture while dancers performed a wedding dance, war dances, and a variety of other dances. The rhythmic music was great and the colorful dancers were impressive. At one point in the night my redneck friend from Alaska was called up onto the stage to dance with the troupe. Rick surprised and amazed us by dancing very well while many of the locals laughed themselves to tears.

Addis Ababa, Ethiopia. 10 January 2011.

Today we went shopping around Churchhill Street looking for silver crosses from the north country and wandered around numerous little shops on the side of a hill. Here we were bugged by a couple of street vendors, but it was just a slight nuisance (or maybe I am just getting used to them). I found a cross I liked set in a dark wood panel with intricate carvings and etched stone pieces but the vendor started at 850 birr (roughly $51 USD) so I walked away.

Next we went to the Piazza neighborhood where silver was sold for 30 birr per gram and I got some silver cuff links for $21. The rectangular cuff links had a silver trim and featured a silver map of Africa set on a black background and weighed 35g.

We ate dinner at the Face of Addis restaurant located on top of a hill with a great view of the city. Unfortunately the food wasn't great and the service was greatly lacking; we had to beg for silverware after the food was delivered two hours after we ordered. After asking for bread four times we got some week-old stale bread, long after we had finished the main course.

Addis Ababa, Ethiopia. 11 January 2011.

This morning we visited the African Union Headquarters and walked around the impressive complex. The Permanent Representative's Committee was in session and we could see the representatives from all over Africa that were sitting behind their desks debating. Most of the people in the art filled corridors were speaking French. My favorite art piece was an intricately carved wooden bust of an African man that was about two feet tall, but unfortunately it was not labeled so I couldn't discover who was the artist or where he came from.

Adjacent to the African Union building the new headquarters buildings were under construction, thanks to the Chinese. The buildings looked amazing even though they were only half way built. Banners in Chinese adorned the skyscraper tower that will easily be the tallest building in Ethiopia. At the foot of the tower is another large globe shaped building that will hold the new assembly chamber. I look forward to visiting again and touring the building when it is completed.

In the afternoon we visited the East African Standby Force and met with the British Peace Support Team for East Africa. The colonel explained how the African Union was structured and interacted for military operations with a Peace and Security Council comprised of a Panel of the Wise, Continental Early Warning System, and the African Standby Force (ASF). The ASF role was to execute observation and monitoring missions, peace support missions, interventions in accordance with the African Union Constitutive Act, to prevent escalation of violence, and demobilization, disarmament, and reintegration (DDR) missions. A key mission was to be able to deploy a robust force within 14 days in response to an emergency. The colonel saw the ASF as a positive force as it could decrease conflict by increasing cooperation between countries and in the overall picture its aim was to prevent regional conflict.

We also visited the Sun Market in Addis to pick up some snacks and found that most of the products were from France or China. Surprisingly they didn't have any milk in a box but had fresh cold milk in a bag. Outside the store we were swarmed by little kids selling Kleenex and chewing gum who jammed their little hands into the car door opening to stop us from closing it. Eventually we were able to get away without anyone getting hurt.

The worst part of driving in Addis is not the lack of traffic rules or signs at almost every intersection, but the people that walk up to your car when stopped in traffic and tap on your windows with their hands out asking for money. If you are stopped for five minutes they will stay there the whole time banging gradually louder on the car and calling out in Amharic. I am surprised that nobody gets hurt with kids and people wandering around in heavy, chaotic traffic.

Djibouti. 12 January 2011.

The morning started with another meeting at the African Union where we met the AFRICOM Commander, General Ward, and the U.S. Ambassador to the African Union for an AMISOM Update. In the AMISOM Update the AU team laid out the sectors in Somalia, disposition of friendly forces, and where operations were taking place to drive out al Shabaab. The AU team briefed a new concept of operations where the AMISOM team would be augmented by more troops and police, however some of the potential troop contributing countries were getting cold feet due to the danger of operating in Somalia. The major challenges identified with AMISOM were finding additional troops and equipment, logistics to move troops and equipment on the battlefield, and non-fulfillment of pledges from African nations.

After the AU meeting we drove to the airport and caught the plane to Djibouti arriving after dark. The short flight from Addis flew over jagged, broken, dusty brown mountains and many milk chocolate dry rivers. The flight was full leaving Addis but more than two-thirds of the passengers disembarked during a brief refueling stop at Dire Dawa, about an hour from Djibouti.

To check into our hotel in Djibouti we had to pass through several different security checkpoints, including getting our baggage screened in an x-ray machine to get inside. We ended up staying at the Djibouti Palace Kempinski upon recommendations of some local friends, mainly for security reasons. The hotel was very expensive but also very comfortable with several swimming pools, good restaurants, a great gym, and the best bed I have slept on in Africa. The bathrooms were amazing with a separate tub and a sauna-shower with an overhead rain shower and bench. But for $250+ USD per night it should be good!

Djibouti. 13 January 2011.

I enjoyed la grasse matinée (sleeping in) thanks to the uber-comfortable bed and the blackout curtain that kept out the brilliant tropical sun. The Kempinski is also located on the outside edge of the port and my room overlooked the pool with a swim-up bar on the edge of the ocean so it was very quiet.

After a quick breakfast at the full breakfast buffet, complete with an omelet chef, we collected our rented Nissan Patrol and headed out to see the city. It was quickly evident that the greater part of the population didn't speak French or English and many of the signs were in Arabic. However, the business class and most of the people we met with were equally competent in English and French and my Franco-handicapped traveling companions were able to communicate very easily.

For the greater part of the local population the day revolved around the noon khat delivery. In the morning the men would work hard to make whatever money he could in order to buy khat, then spend the next couple hours sitting around and chewing the narcotic green leaves talking to friends and enjoying the high. The first 30-45 mins are supposed to make the chewer agitated, but then a cool mellow sets in and the individual chills for the next couple hours. The drug is not illegal and reportedly about 75-80% of the male population chews khat. A friend related that khat is part of the reason for the stability in Djibouti as it keeps the people mellow. If the electricity goes out for two days or there is no water or food prices go up it's not a big deal. However, if there is no khat delivery for two days pandemonium would follow. Accordingly, the state protects and ensures on time delivery of khat every day.

When we returned to the hotel in the early afternoon after exploring we could see groups of men sitting in the shade leaning back and relaxing. The streets that were busy in the morning were now practically deserted, with only a few cars driven by Ferengies (foreigners) on the road.

Later that evening we visited another friend and had dinner with several expat families living in the area. I relished the A&W root beer and cheddar cheese served at dinner, which are very rare commodities in Africa. Over a great dinner of mostly Italian dishes (spaghetti, pesto, bread...) we learned about life for the expat families in Djibouti. With no English-speaking schools in the area all the expat kids attended the French school and the opportunities for recreation for the families were very limited. Most agreed that life in Djibouti was hard for expat families but several had requested extensions to stay longer in the area.

After we said goodbye and headed back to the hotel we were amused by the different sets of guards we passed by who would jump to attention and rush to open the gates to their walled compounds when they saw our headlights. I guess there isn't a lot of traffic after hours in the upscale residential areas.

Djibouti. 14 January 2011.

We woke up early in the morning and ate a rushed breakfast before heading to the port to catch an old wooden Dhow into the Gulf of Aden to swim with Whale Sharks. The Dhow was just like the ones I had traveled on in Qatar years ago. As we drove along the extension to the pier parking lot we saw long lines of men walking to work who started calling out to us as we approached the parking lot. As we made the turn into the parking lot a couple men in ragged clothes pointed to us, then started to run alongside the car with their hands on the door handles and fighting off others to be the one to open the door when we came to a stop. As we got out of the car we were mobbed and our "escorts" would push and shove the others away.

We fought our way through the rocky dirt parking lot and up a narrow gangplank that bowed and flexed considerably under our weight. Once aboard it was evident that we were on the low budget cruise as the cooks started the cooking fire on the main deck in a cut off 55-gallon steel drum. I was glad to see that they had brought jugs of water along to wash their knives and cutting boards as they prepared our lunch on the deck. The cruise on the old leaky diesel boat took over two hours and nearly rattled the fillings out of my teeth. Every half hour someone would turn on the two bilge pumps bolted to the deck to pump out the water accumulating below decks, streaming an unknown amount of water for 10-15 minutes. Stuff streamed out the back of the boat as well from the open bottomed latrine. It seemed that most of the passengers on the ship were from the local French military bases and only a few small kids were aboard. One five-year-old girl amused herself by chasing a kitten around the boat and trying to talk to my English-speaking friends in French.

Finally when we arrived at the western-most point of the Gulf of Aiden the boat dropped anchor near a sandy beach. The crew then brought the two small boats we had towed from the port alongside and began to load the divers. Each of the smaller boats held about 20 passengers and I had the misfortune to get on the second boat that only could move at rowing speed. Unfortunately, two of my friends literally missed the boat and had to stay behind on the mother ship while we crept into the whale shark zone.

The first thing we spotted was a jagged dorsal fin cutting slowly through the water, up to, then under the boat. Once my eyes adjusted I could make out the rows of small white dots that covered the back of the giant shark as it passed under us. While I was still caught up in awe of the giant shark that dwarfed our boat the boatman called out to us to dive. I pulled my mask and snorkel on and fell backwards over the edge of the boat and into the warm blue-green waters teeming with whale sharks and other snorkelers. I watched the first whale shark swim slowly away and turned around just in time to see another massive whale shark coming right at me, only to turn quietly and gently pass me on my right and keep on swimming.

The whale shark is a massive fish that can grow to over 13 meters long and resembles an overgrown catfish without the whiskers. It has over 3000 small teeth but a small mouth and even though I saw it floating and feeding just below the surface of the water I couldn't see what it was eating (must be really small food). I later learned that the whale shark doesn't reach maturity until after 25 years and bears live young (doesn't lay eggs). They are hunted and prized for their fins (for soup), and one whale shark can sell for $10,000 USD. It would not be hard to catch one as they move slowly and I was able to easily swim alongside several in the warm gulf waters. Some of the over eager snorkelers would reach out and touch the whale sharks or try to hold on for a ride, but then the huge gentle animals would dive deeper and disappear from sight leaving the snorkelers gasping for air. We were warned not to touch the whale sharks as it removes the protective mucus from their skin and exposes them to bacteria and causing infection.

The wind and strong currents pushed the whale sharks and us into the back corner of the gulf and I was able to spend over an hour swimming next to, over, under, and around several huge whale sharks. It was amazing just to float behind one as it fed and watch the massive gills open and close as it filtered gallons of water. The water was extremely salty and kept us very buoyant so it was no effort to swim or stay at the surface. The only danger was from the swimming crabs that frequently attacked me and chased me around the area. These hand-sized crabs liked to sneak up behind me and attack my back or hamstrings with their oversized claws so I had to keep turning around to protect my back. It was funny to watch or hear the girlfriends of the French soldiers in the water scream when they got spooked by a whale shark or pinched by a crab.

After about an hour people started to get hungry so we headed back to the mother ship and lunch. Upon reaching the mother ship I jumped in a boat with my two friends that were left behind and headed back to the whale sharks. Natasha had never been snorkeling before and was nervous in the water and the idea of being surrounded by whale sharks. However once she realized it was easy to float and got used to having her head in the water she quickly joined in the chase and enjoyed swimming with the sharks.

Lunch when we got back on the boat was meat on a skewer, a vegetable salad in mayonnaise, french bread, rice, and a red stew. Once everyone had eaten we began the long three-hour cruise back against the strengthening wind and rising seas. The wind swells would pitch the bow twenty feet in the air as we slowly pushed our way across the great troughs of water. At one point one of the two smaller boats broke free and we had to circle back to get it.   Later we had to circle back again when the wind swept a pile of unused life vests into the sea. I became bored and laid down on the deck and fell asleep to the vibrating massage of the rickety diesel engine and the bilge pumps continuously pumping water from the hold.

I woke up as we entered the calm of the harbor, refreshed from a day in the sun and warm ocean. Back onshore we gathered our gear we returned to the car and paid our private vehicle security guard, he didn't look like he cared anymore- his eyes were glazed over as he chewed on mouthful of green khat leaves, and returned to the luxury hotel for the night.

Djibouti. 15 January 2011.

No visit to Djibouti is complete without visiting the only U.S. military base on the African Continent: Camp Lemonnier. The base is adjacent to the international airport, on the far side of the flight line from the international terminal. In fact, passengers waiting for their flights can watch American military aircraft take off from hangers under a massive American flag. While the rest of Djibouti is a light brownish-tan color, like yellow sand, inside the Hesco walls of the U.S. base all is the color of the crushed gray gravel and gray Hesco walls. The base, Camp Lemonnier, used to be a French Foreign Legion military outpost but was acquired by the U.S. following 9-11 in order to give the American troops a Launchpad for operations into the Middle East to fight terrorist groups.

Camp Lemonnier has also been used to coordinate anti-piracy missions and the Combined Joint Task Force- Horn of Africa (CJTF-HOA) was established there in 2004 to fight terrorist groups in the region. CJTF-HOA now has the role of supporting African Union troops attempting to defeat al-Shabaab and stabilize Somalia. Over

3000 U.S. military troops are based at Camp Lemonnier and the base is complete with a dining facility, multiple gyms, a theater, a pizza shop, subway sandwich shop, small pool, and a Green Bean coffee shop. It was a flashback to Bagram Air Force Base in Afghanistan to see the troops in their gray uniforms walking in the dusty gray gravel and drinking the exact same coffee brand.

The main difference from Afghanistan was that in Djibouti we weren't getting rocketed or mortared on a daily basis and when the troops left the base they weren't going on combat patrols. It was slightly surreal that just a couple days ago I was nearby snorkeling with whale sharks and wandering around downtown while this fully armed American combat base was postured and prepared for a fight like in Afghanistan or Iraq.

During our visit to the base we were briefed on combat operations in Somalia, how AMISOM (African Union Mission in Somalia) troops were fighting al-Shabaab and what CJTF-HOA was doing to support and assist operations. However, Djibouti city seemed like most other sleepy African desert towns.

For dinner we visited a restaurant located on the 4th floor of a building downtown that provided a panoramic view of the city and it's many lights. The food was alright, but they only offered French cuisine. During the four days we spent in Djibouti the only local food we were able to find was on the boat trip, as it seemed the restaurants that were recommended to us only served Italian or French food.

Nairobi, Kenya. 16-19 January 2011.

Traffic in Nairobi sucks. It seems like the greater part of the roads in the city are under construction so it takes hours to get from the airport to downtown or anywhere else in the city. The major road projects affecting traffic are the construction of a new bridge near downtown and a series of underpasses to replace the jammed traffic circles (or roundabouts) where we sat for hours in our taxis.

For the work portion of our trip we visited the U.S. Embassy and met with the Defense Attaché and discussed U.S. military engagement in the region. The U.S. Mission to Kenya was the largest in sub-Saharan Africa and Kenya was the seventh largest recipient of U.S. foreign assistance worldwide and had the fifth largest PEPFAR (President's Urgent Plan for AIDS Relief) program. Kenya was also a participant in the ACOTA (African Contingency Operations Training and Assistance) program, like many of the other African countries I had visited so far (also Senegal, Ghana, Nigeria, Tanzania, Djibouti, Ethiopia, and Zambia). The Kenya office also covered Somalia and South Sudan.

While we were in Nairobi we were able to do a number of activities: visit a shopping center where we watched Tron Legacy (a great movie from the U.S.), ate lunch at the United Nations headquarters, and played a round of golf at the Windsor Hotel and Golf Resort. The UN compound was huge with organizations represented by every set of letters you could jumble together. The people seemed busy but a friend who worked in the area commented that most of them spend their time in the pool or gym. We checked it out and the gym was very nice and offered yoga, Zumba, and spinning classes and featured new equipment. The food at the UN cafeteria was great too.

Golf at the Windsor was great and the caddies who carried our rented clubs found most of the balls we lost. The scenery was awesome but sometimes you had to wait for the monkeys to clear the green so you could chip or putt. On the ninth hole as we approached the green by the hotel my second shot was attacked by a group of large raptors who kept trying to steal my ball and fly away. Bird after large bird would swoop down and pick up my ball and fly several feet before losing their grip and dropping it again. Unfortunately they were flying towards me and not towards the green! So my next shot was several yards further out than it should have been, but we weren't playing for money, just enjoying the awesome experience of playing golf in Kenya.

Mombasa, Kenya. 19-21 January 2011.

The first thing I learned in Mombasa, Kenya is that the rental car companies, particularly Budget Rental Car, have no internet connection so if you forgot to bring your contract that you set up online you are out of luck. The second thing is that that I learned is that the car you get probably won't be the car you reserved. We rented a small SUV and ended up with an old beat up RAV-4 with 166,000km that was falling apart. The car belonged to the cousin of the person who worked behind the Budget counter and hooked us up with a "special" deal. It took about half an hour to annotate all the damage to the vehicle on the rental form before we could leave. The third thing I learned right away in Mombasa, Kenya is that since we were borrowing the family car, we had family responsibilities, like we had to drop off the owner of the car at his house since he was so nice as to bring the car to the airport for us. Luckily I didn't make the car reservation, so my friend who did got to go through the aggravation of working it all out and then driving through town to the hotel. The fourth thing we learned is that there are no maps; Budget didn't have any and we didn't bring any with us. The welcome desk was kind enough to give us a map of Kenya but nobody had any idea where the hotel was located besides saying it was on the North Coast. Eventually we found it after some extended exploring and turning down nearly every side street on the road north.

We got a pretty good package deal at the Serena Hotel (located some 30km from the airport) that included breakfast and buffet dinners and I ate too much. The food was good and we spent the first couple days working off the extra weight by scuba diving, lounging, or exploring Haller Park. My friend Natasha, who had just tried snorkeling for the first time with the whale sharks in Djibouti, completed her PADI Open Water Certification in two and a half days by studying all night, doing pool dives in the morning, and open water dives in the afternoon. She did very well and was excited to dive Zanzibar the following month!

However, I got bent. We did two dives and broke all the scuba rules and completely blew the dive tables when we followed the plan of the Assistant Dive Master. The Dive Master was the European figurehead for the PADI School and was never around. He refused to go on a dive with us and it seemed that he just allowed the Kenyans to use his name to run the program. I was dumb and just followed the assistant dive masters even when they told us not to worry about breaking the rules. The first cardinal rule we broke was to dive deep first. We dove 20 meters for 36 minutes, but then dove again in less than 30 minutes. For the second dive we dove 24 meters for 37 minutes, when according to the dive tables, we should have only gone to that depth for 9 minutes, if that, after such a short surface interval.

During the short break between dives I felt terrible. The tiny pitching boat on the open sea outside the protective barrier reef made my face turn green and I was holding on for my dear life so I didn't question the uber-short surface interval- I just wanted to get back in the water so I would feel better. I did feel better for a bit but after 10-15 minutes on the bottom (around 24 meters) my nausea came back again and I felt like taking out my regulator and puking. The fun had gone out of the dive and my field of vision narrowed. I didn't care about the huge sea turtles swimming by or the white tipped reef sharks we found at the end, I just wanted out of the water and to get back on shore. Out of the water I felt better, but back on shore I struggled to rinse and put my gear away and then shuffled back to my room to take a nap. Mild headaches kept me from sleeping and I watched a movie with my dive buddy Rick who was also having some blurred vision. I thought it was just the continuation of being seasick and stayed in bed for the rest of the night.

Rick says we made a skype video call to our Rescue Diver friend, Stu, in Italy but I don't remember it as much of the afternoon was a blur. Apparently Stu confirmed the bends and recommended that since there were no recompression chambers within several hundred miles of Mombasa that we rest and drink water. Getting into a hyperbaric recompression chamber would have fixed the nitrogen gas bubble problems that we were experiencing and is the only lifesaving treatment in the more serious cases of the bends.

The next day the mild headaches came and went as we explored Haller Park, a limestone quarry that was converted into a wildlife park in the 70s. It cost about $10 USD to enter the park and a guide took us around to see the giraffes, the hippos who were hiding, the fish farm, and the snake house. Really it was an overgrown zoo, but it was still admirable that they had turned a pit into an ecosystem with ponds, circulating water, and imported animals. I felt like crap again after walking around the park for an hour or two and decided to skip the afternoon dive with Natasha and Rick, and that decision could have saved my life. While I rested I tried to calculate the pressure groups for my dive log and the online calculators kept saying there was an error with the dive. So I did the numbers using the PADI dive tables and it became apparent that the second dive was stupid and dangerous.

Resolutions: (1) Join DAN just in case I am diving and something goes wrong they can get me help or get me to a hyperbaric chamber. (2) Buy a good dive computer that will help me calculate my pressure groups. (3) Don't just accept what the dive master tells me- double check the plan and don't dive stupid!

Mombasa, Kenya. 22 January 2011.

Mombasa is famous for its great beaches and for its deep-water ports. Because of the port and its strategic location near hot spots like Somalia, Sudan, and Rwanda, the World Food Program located its East African Headquarters and warehouse facilities in Mombasa. Ships pull into the port and load food directly onto trucks for a long drive to their final destination in Somalia, Sudan, Ethiopia, Rwanda, Burundi, DRC, and Uganda or the food is stored in the port warehouse or a series of other warehouses in the area. The World Food Program in Mombasa was the transit point for over 355,000 metric tons of food in 2010.

Yesterday we toured the Mombasa port facility while a ship from the United States was unloading sacks of cornmeal. In the WFP warehouse we saw hundreds of palates of cooking oil and split peas from USAID awaiting delivery. The warehouse also held tons of peanut paste in squeeze tubes from France and other foods donated by other countries around the world. One section was covered by a tarp and was being fumigated to kill any potential bugs, as the delivery to the warehouse took longer than expected.

The hard or dangerous part of the job for the World Food Program is the delivery to the final destination, often a refugee camp or some other austere location where people are starving. Only certain personnel are allowed to go on delivery missions and they are often accompanied by armed escorts. About 2% of the shipments never make it to their final destination due to robbers, hijackings, or accidents. The World Food Program forbids the resale of donated food but it can often be found in stores or shacks for sale, without any penalty to the seller. It was interesting to find WFP labeled food in shops elsewhere in Africa and contemplate the journey the food took to get to some very remote places.

7 KILIMANJARO

Moshi, Tanzania, 23 January 2011 (Kilimanjaro Day 0)

The team gathered from all over Africa, arriving in Moshi, Tanzania to prepare for the seven-day attempt to summit Kilimanjaro, the highest mountain in Africa at 19,100 ft. We hired the expedition company Ultimate Kilimanjaro, who subcontracted to Zara Tours for the expedition. The first to arrive at the lodge were Brian and his wife Chandra from Botswana, Rick from Mozambique, myself from Senegal, Natasha and Lubna from Ethiopia, and Stu from Italy. Natasha, Rick, and I flew directly from diving in Mombasa to the slopes of Kilimanjaro. Later that evening Jason from DRC and Jake from Virginia arrived to complete the team.

Bags were weighed and gear separated before we met our guide, Chombo, at the lodge for the briefing on the trek. Our group would consist of the nine-team members, supported by three porters each, our guide, two assistant guides, a cook, and an assistant cook (full expedition strength: 41 people- 32 staff and 9 customers). The porters would carry the tents, food and other gear as well as up to 15kg per customer. They would travel ahead of us and set up camp and start cooking so when we arrived everything would be ready and we could sit down and enjoy some hot chocolate/tea/coffee and popcorn as well as the view.

Machame Camp, 24 January 2011 (Kilimanjaro Day 1)

I got up three hours before start time to double-check my packs and to ensure I had everything on the packing list. I started taking Diamox (drug that helps your blood carry more oxygen at altitude) the night before and I was already starting to experience the side effect, a weird tingling sensation in my hands, as I made my final preparations. The hotel specializes in Kilimanjaro expeditions and offers a storage room where I stashed my "stay behind" bag with all the stuff I didn't need for the climb.

The bus and guides showed up at 9am and we drove 45 minutes from the hotel to the Machame Gate (altitude 1500m or 5,921 feet) where our guides had to register us for the climb and pay the fees. At the gate we ate our sack lunches and bought some last minute gear from locals who sold stuff through the gate. I picked up a pair of Gore-Tex gaiters for $20, which were previously donated to guides by their former patrons.

At 11am we started the long upward trek to the summit of Kilimanjaro. The walk begins by walking up a series of ridgelines through a tropical rainforest and we were fortunate to stay dry for the first five hours. Sunglasses and hats weren't needed with the thick tree canopy and we spent the beginning hours getting used to our 10kg loads (including 3 liters of water, snacks, rain gear, and whatever else you wanted to carry) and the continuous stream of porters that flowed past. The temptation was to keep up with the porters or pass them back, but the guides repeated their mantra "Pole Pole" or "slowly slowly." I hate Pole Pole, but was thankful, as the altitude was already hurting my lungs and pushing my heart rate.

We ate lunch on the side of the trail and watched some monkeys swinging from tree to tree. Besides the monkeys there wasn't much to see besides trees, other groups, and thousands of porters carrying huge loads on their heads and shoulders. The rain at the end of the day made the trail slick but cooled off the tropical heat in the forest.

17km and 7 hours after we started we arrived at Machame Camp (elevation 2980m or 9776 feet) as the sun set, soaked to the skin, and tired. We signed into the camp office as the rain intensified, then trudged to our two-man dome tents to drop our packs and change into dry clothes. I felt much better in a dry shirt and joined the group in the dining tent for some popcorn and "Milo," a powdered chocolate drink like Nestle Quik. An hour later, huge plates of potatoes and soup were served for dinner. There were also some boiled vegetables and some form of burnt fish that we tried to choke down. Outside we had a smaller tent that housed a small porta-pottie that got lugged from camp to camp during our trip. After dinner we crashed early to the peaceful pitter-patter sound of rain on the tent.

Shira Camp, 25 January 2011 (Kilimanjaro Day 2)

The rain stopped during the night and in the morning the clouds already had formed a floor that blocked the view beneath the forest. We had some porridge for breakfast and shouldered our packs to start up the hill. As we exited the camp the rain forest gave way to misty heather with many large bushes. We were thankful as the trail changed from the rich loam of the forest to more of a gravel trail that wasn't as slippery.

As we walked we were continuously enveloped in passing clouds. It was hard to tell time in the clouds and the 9km scheduled for the day went by quickly. The walking wasn't hard and there were only a few places near the end of the day where we had to put the trekking poles away in order to use our hands to climb over a rock escarpment onto the Shira plateau. It took us six hours to get to Shira Camp at 3840m (12,598 ft) and when the clouds broke we had an amazing view of the plains below and the summit above. It didn't look that far away but we still had another four days of walking to get to the top.

We got into camp early in order to allow ourselves time to acclimatize and try to avoid altitude sickness. Most of our crew lives at sea level so we were concerned and took Diamox as a precaution. However, one member of the group was unable to take Diamox due to a sulpha-allergy and took Viagra instead (his trail name).

Since we had some time to kill I wandered around our huge encampment. There were hundreds of tents set up over the side of the mountain and I heard many different languages and accents I didn't recognize. Next to our camp was a bunch of Germans who were taking baths in the open with cold water. On the other side was a luxury group of girls with video cameras doing a documentary about climbing the three highest points in Africa over a three-week period. Further down the slope was the porter camp, which was the loudest and most colorful of all, and where our food was cooked.

Dinner was more potatoes and some kind of meat accompanied by potato-leek soup. The cold wind blowing across the exposed plain where we camped kept the temperatures cool and during the night water left outside froze.

Barranco Camp, 26 January 2011 (Kilimanjaro Day 3)

I didn't enjoy the potatoes too much last night (our theory about the constant potatoes was that the porters didn't want to carry them anymore so they fed us a steady diet of potatoes) and didn't wake up very hungry. I couldn't eat the eggs they offered for breakfast but I had a glass of Milo and we hit the trail. Chambo, our guide, warned us that today was going to be a hard day, as we would go high and camp low.

We followed our guides as we were continually passed by porters along the Shira route up to the Lava Tower at 4630m (15,190 feet) and down the other side. I felt pretty good as we climbed the trail to the tower so I disregarded Chombo's advice to get off the tower quickly and spent some time climbing some boulders and taking pictures. As we came down from the tower I started to get a headache at the base of my skull that gradually increased and I completely lost my appetite. At lunch I tried to choke down some peanuts and bread but couldn't eat anything else.

Seven hours after we set out we reached Barranco Camp at 3950m (12,959 feet) and I was suffering. I was barely putting one foot in front of the other and had severe tunnel vision. It hurt to lift my head so I just trudged along at the end of the line until I tumbled into my tent. I immediately fell asleep and woke up to "Billy Goat" (Rick's trail name) checking on me since I disappeared as soon as we got into camp. He tried to get me to eat something but instead I started to throw up, luckily outside the tent. After I puked I felt much better, drank some water, and fell asleep for four hours.

I woke up for dinner and the nausea was gone and the headache had diminished some so I ate some porridge for dinner with Camelbak Elixir electrolyte drink and went back to bed. While I was eating a member of the Canadian party that was following us came by looking for a doctor. A lady in the group was also sick, but much worse. It turns out they were told that an Advil a day would be enough to counter the effects of the altitude. They were painfully mistaken and she had to climb down in the morning.

Karanga Camp, 27 January 2011 (Kilimanjaro Day 4)

After a good 10 hours of sleep I woke up feeling great! The nausea and headaches were gone and I was hungry again! I ate three bowls of porridge as we got the brief for the days trek: a short day, but with a lot of scrambling. We would first have to scale the Great Barranco Wall, then cross over the ridge to sleep at the new camp, but again at about the same elevation as the current camp.

We tried to start late in order to allow the porters to get their heavy burdens through the narrow bottlenecks and overhead climbs but we still got stuck in the mix. The Great Barranco Wall is a narrow trail up a 600-meter cliff face where if you slip you will plunge to your death in the rocky stream below. One of our porters climbing ahead of us slipped and tumbled to the edge but hung on while his bag sailed off the cliff. We were all glad to see he was ok but all the other porters whistled at him the whole way as he had to run back down the narrow trail to pick up the bag and back up to catch up with the group (the bag held Chombo's tent).

Once past the wall the trail opened up again and we crossed many glacial streams, passed freezing waterfalls, and traversed several wide sandy fields. The surviving member of a Canadian group joined us on the trail as the rest of her group had gone down early in the morning due to the altitude sickness. We were now above the cloud layer and the sun began to burn us as we walked. SPF 50 couldn't stop the sun's rays from burning my neck so I had to use my Afghan handkerchief as a scarf (as "Arnie of Africa").

The walk was easy until we got to the final kilometer leading to the Karanga Camp, where a chasm like the Grand Canyon opened before us. It would have been the perfect place for an Indiana Jones style rope bridge as a narrow stream had cut a steep valley at least 200 meters deep. Instead we had to descend carefully the steep canyon walls; sliding down some exposed rock slabs to the bottom and then slowly crawl up a trail with many, many switchbacks. At the top we were rewarded with our campsite and a great view of the summit that was slowly approaching.

We camped at 3963m (13,001 feet) and the steady wind kept it cold and shook the tent all night. I was grateful for the 0*F down sleeping bag I had bought just for the trip. The water froze again during the night but I had to unzip the bag because I was overheating!

Barafu Camp, 28 January 2011 (Kilimanjaro Day 5)

We had opted for the 7-day climb instead of the more common 6-day climb along the Machame Route in order to give us an extra day of acclimatization. When we stopped at the Karanga Camp last night many others pushed on to Barafu Camp at 4550m (14,927 ft). This allowed us to take it easy on day five, to sleep in a little, and only have to walk for three hours. Last night we played 19 hands of Hearts (won by "Viagra") and today after our short walk we played two games of 13 and 14 hands each (won by "G4 Challenge" and "Pooter").

The trail to Barafu camp was steep and traversed many scree covered slopes and sand fields. We all felt pretty good and were amazed at the views that surrounded us. Surprisingly we never ran out of stuff to talk about while other groups around us were melting down and people were being threatened with trekking pole stabbings. Our guides kept us going "Pole Pole" and we trudged along, becoming more excited as we got ever closer to the top.

At the end of the trail, we arrived at the last camp before the summit on a rocky exposed ridge with steep drops off either side. A set of permanent latrines hung over the side of a cliff face and the porters stayed in green colored round metal shacks. We, however, slept in our blue little dome tents with a relentless howling wind that threatened to launch our tents off the ridge.

We ate an early dinner and went to bed before 7pm because the next day, and the final assault on the summit, would begin at 11:30pm.

Barafu Camp, 28 January 2011 (Kilimanjaro Day 6)

I slept well for about two hours then put on all my gear and fought through the wind to link up with the group in the dinner tent. I wore medium-weight polypro tights underpants and Gore-Tex hard-shell snow bibs for my lower body. On my upper body I wore a polypro top, fleece pullover, and puff jacket and carried my Gore-Tex hard-shell jacket in my pack. I filled my camelbak with three liters of Camelbak Elixer drink and carried two snickers bars for energy (I can't stand Powerbars or Clifbars anymore- I have reached my lifetime limit). I also carried spare batteries for my headlamp, which came in handy for "Trailbait" when her headlamp died three hours into the climb.

It was dark, cold, and windy when we stepped off at 11:45pm. Normally its 20*F at the camp but the 30mph wind gusts froze my insulated Camelbak in my backpack solid by 2:30am. We started "Pole Pole," just one foot in front of the other, in the frigid dark. The headlamps only illuminated the way for six to ten feet so we just watched the back or the feet of the person in front of you. We only took three breaks of five minutes each on the way to the top as everyone was too cold to be stationary for very long.

Around 2:20am a blood-red horseshoe of a crescent moon rose above the horizon below us. The stars around us didn't give enough light to see our surroundings. Down in the distance below us we could see the lights of many small towns. We just kept moving, six inches forward per step as the incline increased over steep scree and sand covered slopes. I don't remember too much as I tried to go to my "happy place" as the hours of climbing went by.

As we got closer to the top under the thin light of the moon I could make out the edge of the horizon before us and the glaciers around us. Around 5am we made it to the rim of the crater and turned left. I was at the end of the group, breathing like I was running the last bit of a marathon, with my heart beating four times for every breath. When I slowed my breathing the headache at the base of my skull would set in, so I tried Lamaze breathing like I was having a baby.

At 5:50am we made it to the rickety wooden sign that said we were at the highest point in Africa: Uhuru Peak at 5896m (19,343 feet). As we gathered in front of the sign for victory picture the first sliver of red light pierced the cloud-covered horizon below us. Headaches began to assault us as we stood at the top so I split with a small group to get down "Haraka Haraka" (quickly quickly).

As we descended the morning light illuminated the dirty white & blue glacier fields we had passed in the night. The views were awesome, but I couldn't stop to take any pictures; my head was killing me and it was too damn cold. It took us six hours to get to the top, but we descended the 5,000 feet in an hour. The best part of the descent was the 1000 vertical feet of a scree field that I bounded down in small leaps. Besides that, the consensus of the group was that it was good that we ascended in the dark of the night because the steepness of the slope was ridiculous.

We were the first group to make it to the top and we blew by the groups on the way downhill that had sped by us on the lower elevations earlier in the week. Our "Pole Pole" guides had got us into a rhythm that carried us to the top, with 100% success- all nine of us made it to the summit. Back at camp I quickly shucked my gear and thawed my Camelbak for a quick drink before taking a nap. After lunch we had another 5,000 vertical feet to descend to get to the camp for the night.

Mweka Camp, 29 January 2011 (Kilimanjaro Day 6.2)

I awoke from my nap refreshed, but still with a mild dull headache. Several members of the group puked on the way down from the summit and now we were in a hurry to get lower. Going up may be hard, but I think descending can be more painful. Especially when you descend 5,000 vertical feet in less than five hours.

The alpine scree and boulder fields gradually gave way to heather and scrub brush as we descended a ridgeline trail. By the end of the day we were back in the rain forest, but luckily it wasn't raining. The constant downhill pounding numbed my two big toes (different than the Diamox tingling that would affect your hands, feet, and face) but in the seven-day trek no one in the group had any blisters.

"Billy Goat" celebrated back in camp with Kilimanjaro beers, a bottle of Jack Daniels, and cigars while I downed a Sprite, more Milo, and popcorn. I was glad to sleep on flat ground again and everyone felt much better below 10,000ft. Worn out from the day, everyone crashed early and slept soundly through the night.

While we descended we passed groups who shared some bad news from the mountain. The night we reached the summit a man died from altitude sickness and two others broke their legs and had to be carried off the mountain. The fatality was a man who started the climb sick, and against medical advice, decided to sleep on the mountain despite acute altitude sickness. Our group was very fortunate that we all summited and descended without any injury or problems beside mild altitude sickness. Usually once we puked we felt better!

Moshi, Tanzania: Kili Day 7, 30 January 2011

For the last day of our Kilimanjaro Trek I had mixed feelings. On one hand I couldn't wait to get off the mountain, but on the other hand I had a lot of fun and really enjoying walking around the mountain with my friends and didn't want it to end. On summit day I would have told you that my new definition of hell was being stuck on the face of Kilimanjaro four hours into the climb with a frozen Camelbak and two more hours of climbing ahead of you. Looking back on it two weeks later from the comfort of my warm apartment in Dakar I would do it again.

We leisurely descended the mountain under the canopy of the rain forest, the mountain hidden by the thick trees. It took us three hours to get to the Mweka Gate where we ate a quick lunch while being harassed by locals selling t-shirts and bracelets. An hour later we were back at the hotel where we cleaned up before jumping in the pool. Later we linked up with our Canadian friends and went out to dinner and the next morning we went our separate ways again.

Big thanks to Chombo, our guide from Zara Tours, for getting us up and down the mountain safely. I am particularly grateful he helped me through my altitude sickness and that he judged me well enough to continue, all the way to the top.

Trail Names:

Natasha: "Trail Bait" because everyone that met her would hit on her and ask for her number. The bolder men would ask her to marry them.

Stu: "Viagra" as he has a sulfa allergy that required him to use Viagra to deal with the altitude instead of Diamox like the rest of us.

Rick: "Billy Goat" because he would often bound off the trail and climb some rocks to get a better view.

Chandra: "G-Force Challenge" as that was written in huge letters across her jacket.

Lubna: "Pooter" earned her name due to frequent flatulence.

Jake: "the Snake." not very original.

Brian: "Westy," an old nick-name that stuck with him.

Jason: "Slim Jeans," named for his slick Patagonia soft-shell pants.

Arnie: "Arnie of Africa" due to my Afghan scarfs to hide from the scorching sun (think Lawrence of Arabia).

8 RWANDA & BURUNDI

Kigali, Rwanda: 2 February 2011.

After a week at the highest point in Africa, we immediately retreated to sea level at Dar es Salaam for a couple days before the next trip. Here the group split up and I continued on with Brad to Rwanda and Burundi. Brad and I caught the early flight from Dar Es Salaam at 5:10am to Kigali via Nairobi on 2 Feb and gained an hour as we moved into Central African Time. The hills in Rwanda were amazing as we flew into Kigali and a light rain met us on the ground.

We had a lot of preconceptions or ideas on what to expect in Rwanda from reading lots of books about the genocide and complaints about the fairness of the last elections, but Rwanda has been a weirdly pleasant experience. We were surprised when the customs people in the airport didn't speak French but English, and I was taken aback when the plastic bag wrapping my duffle bag full of gear from Kilimanjaro was confiscated. It turns out that plastic bags are banned in Rwanda in order to protect the environment, which is a great idea in my opinion because too many African country sides are littered by torn bits of blue and black plastic bags. I wish more countries would consider doing the same.

Once out of the airport and on our way to the hotel I was amazed to see clean streets! There was no litter to be seen and squads of locals were painting the curbs an alternating black and white pattern and the city seemed brand new. Even the roads were freshly paved and smooth. The next thing that caught my attention was that the city was very quiet. The cacophony of honking horns, loud music, and roaring crowds usually found in African capitals was missing in Kigali. Even the people I talked to on the street spoke in hushed voices almost like living in a library.

At the embassy we were briefed that Rwanda was considered a development success, had a low AIDS rate (thanks to PEPFAR), and wanted to become a regional peacekeeping operations training site. Rwanda was a part of the ACOTA training program and was contributing peacekeeping troops to Sudan and other peacekeeping missions.

One of the reasons we had scheduled our visit to Rwanda for the beginning of February is that a unit from the Kansas National Guard was in town to work with a Rwandan Peacekeeping Battalion under ACOTA and we were able to go out to the training site and observe the training. We met with the American trainers and the Rwandan officers and watched a machine gun range and Rwandans conducting a land-navigation course. We then went to the exercise command post and watched how the battalion staff reacted to simulated attacks and repositioned supplies and forces. Next we were given a tour of the training base, which had great training facilities with a mortar range complete with decommissioned vehicles as hard targets, patrol lanes with checkpoint scenarios, and a forward operating base. The facilities were well developed with concrete tent pads and brick and mortar latrines, some of the nicest military latrines I had seen in Africa.

We were fortunate to be booked the Hotel Milles Colines, the famous Hotel Rwanda from the Oscar winning movie. I had recently watched the movie and expected something different, riddled with bullet holes and other damages from the war but the hotel was in great shape. It wasn't the same as in the movie, but was definitely a high-class hotel with a nice pool, bar, and good rooms. Another unexpected discovery was that the street vendors were selling "the Economist" or "Jeune Afrique" magazines at the hotel gate instead of the usual crowd in other cities that sold cell phone minute cards or the local papers. The free wifi was greatly appreciated as I surfed the net as I watched the sunset poolside.

Kigali, Rwanda. 3 February 2011

Breakfast is served on the fourth floor of Hotel Milles Colines, which provides a stunning panoramic view of the hills of Kigali at sunrise. The view is amazing and the city is beautiful. After breakfast we walked over to the Rwandan National Parks office and managed to score two passes to the National Park on the Ugandan border to go look for gorillas! Only 56 people are allowed in the park each day and usually the passes, which cost $500 USD each, sell out months in advance. But today there were two cancellations so my friend Brad and I were able to get passes for the following day.

For the gorilla trek we would have to travel to the Virunga mountains on the northern Rwandan border and meet the guides at the Karisoke Research Center. Dr. Dian Fossey founded the Karisoke Research Center in 1967 and spent the rest of her life studying and protecting the local mountain gorilla populations.

Once we had the passes in hand we went back to the hotel and booked two nights at an ecolodge just outside the park, rented a rusty Toyota Landcruiser (driver included), and headed north. The old Landcruiser struggled and groaned up the steep hills leaving Kigali and rattled down the few rough sections where the road wasn't paved, but we finally arrived three hours later. The views were awe inspiring as we drove through the Rwandan countryside and I could easily see how others had called Rwanda the "Garden of Eden."

On our drive across Rwanda we drove through many small towns and villages where the people were lining up to vote in local elections. One method for voting was for the candidates to stand in a line and face away from the crowd and the supporters would then line up behind the candidate they supported. The candidates were not allowed to look until the vote was complete.

At one point a convoy of black Cadillac Escalades blew by us and the driver noted that the President was going to one of the villages for the election. The roads in the countryside were as clean, freshly paved and painted as in the city. There were also yellow fiber optic cable junction boxes every few kilometers along the roadside. We also frequently saw men, women, and children carrying large yellow five-gallon jugs. The driver said the women and children were carrying water in their jugs but the men had banana beer in theirs.

Near the national park we caught up with a Chinese road construction crew that the driver said, "work day and night, day and night" with little rest. We saw a Chinese foreman nearly a hundred locals working with shovels to clear the side of the road. In a change from other countries we also saw Rwandans driving the trucks and steamrollers and operating the heavy equipment instead of Chinese workers. I was also surprised to see that the construction flaggers who controlled traffic around the work crew also had women controlling traffic.

Despite checkpoints every ten kilometers we made good time and turned off from the main road 25km from the Ugandan border to drive up the mountain to the ecolodge.

We booked a cabin through Volcanoes Safaris for a small eight-cabin eco-resort that was totally off the grid and situated on a hilltop overlooking several lakes and volcanos on the Ugandan border. Solar panels and a windmill powered the resort and solar tanks heated the water. Unfortunately, there was no Wi-Fi, but it was an all-inclusive resort with drinks, meals, massages, everything included in the price.

We first had drinks by the fireplace in the main lodge and later the other campers, who hailed from Chicago, Vancouver, Victoria Island, and Holland, joined us at dinner in the dining room. All were excited to go on the Gorilla trek in the morning and this was everyone's first trip to Africa.

Virunga, Rwanda. 4 February 2011

Exactly at 5am, there was a knock at the door. It was the porter with the morning hot chocolate and a biscuit which I hastily drank as I got my pack ready for the day searching for gorillas in the mist. Breakfast was served in the dining room 30 minutes later and then we were on our way, bumping down the rocky dirt road into the snowy mist below from our hilltop resort (elevation 2100m or 6,890ft).

We rendezvoused with the other gorilla seekers at the park headquarters and were broken into groups of eight and introduced to our guides. Francis, our guide, said we were lucky to visit the Sabyinyo troop, which featured the largest silverback gorilla in the park. From the park we drove another 45 minutes, the last 20 minutes of which was driving up a rocky creek bed. I said a silent prayer when the engine stalled as the badly beaten Landcruiser heaved around a boulder, and fortunately the battered car wheezed back to life with some gentle coaxing from the driver.

The drivers stayed with the vehicles when we reached the end of the trail and we set out on foot across the green fields on the side of a volcano, accompanied by our guide, a couple trackers with radios, and our two armed escorts carrying AK-47 assault rifles. Francis gave us a final briefing before we jumped over the rock wall that separated the fields from the mountain jungle above. He warned to us to turn off the flash on our cameras and keep quiet no matter what, even if we rolled in the prolific stinging nettle or covered with giant biting ants.

Francis asserted that it was better to suffer in silence than to spook the gorillas (because they might get aggressive and charge).

Over the wall, huge black ants attacked the first man in line but he kept quiet. We then threaded our way through a bamboo forest following the trackers, slipping in the ankle deep mud and occasionally falling into stinging nettle. We continued on in silence for 20 minutes until we broke into a clearing where Francis told us to drop our bags and grab our cameras because the gorillas were near. Across the clearing we could see the tops of the giant bamboo sway, one by one, followed by a loud snap as the plant disappeared.

A tracker took the lead, machete in hand, and disappeared as he ducked under some broken bamboo, closely followed by the first man in the group. I was the last man to step into the darkness and followed up a steep incline to where the group was stopped. At first I only saw the huge piles of gorilla poop, but then I looked to where everyone else was staring in stunned silence. An enormous furry black hand reached out of a nest of bamboo branches, grabbed a stalk about four inches across, snapped it off, and started shoving the tender leaves into his mouth. The 500 lb. silverback looked over at us, paused for a second, then went back to chewing his mouthful of leaves. Slowly the photographers in the group raised their cameras and tentatively took their first shots. The gorilla was only ten feet away but didn't seem to mind us watching him closely. Unlike the zoo there was nothing to stop the giant gorilla from dropping down from his bamboo hammock and ripping our limbs off. But he just went on chewing leaves, and eventually rolled off his perch and walked away.

The guide only allowed us one hour with the gorillas in order to protect them from too much exposure to humans and the diseases we carry so a tracker quickly led us to another group of gorillas under the bamboo boughs. As we moved into position to take some photos a baby and a medium-sized gorilla shot past us, nearly knocking me over. The giant silverback slowly followed them right by us, close enough to feel his breath, up to a small clearing where they sat down and began to strip off and eat the leaves off the stinging nettle.

We stood around and took pictures only five feet away from the small family and the hour quickly passed. Reluctantly we packed up our cameras and slipped down the muddy slope to where the armed guards watched over our bags, tipped them, and walked back to our trucks. Less than an hour later we were back at the super ecolodge, where our muddy boots were collected for cleaning and shining.

Later in the evening school kids from the local village came up to the lodge and performed a series of traditional dances. The boys swung wooden spears and wore long blond headdresses, and the girls danced with baskets on their heads. They danced and sang about their ancient traditions of farming and herding in the high hills of Rwanda. At the end they were joined by their teacher who serenaded us on a local multiple stringed instrument as he sang about the green volcanoes that encircled us, the two lakes on either side of the village below where we sat, and also gave thanks for the ecolodge and asked us to tell our friends to come visit soon. After tipping heavily we went back to the dining room for dinner then back to the cabin to our beds with visions of gorillas and kids with spears dancing in our heads.

Kigali, Rwanda. 5 February 2011

During our last day in Kigali we stopped at the Kigali Memorial Center and saw some of the horrors of the massacres in Rwanda. Over 250,000 Rwandans are buried on the site and it was a very emotional visit for our driver who took us to the site. He had lost most of his family and he was struggling to forgive and move on.

On the drive to the museum our driver pointed out where a machine gun had been set overwatching an intersection in downtown Kigali during the genocide and many people were killed. He also showed us where checkpoints had been set up and people killed for being from the wrong ethnic group. I thought it was interesting that our driver refused to tell us if he was Hutu or Tutsi and only repeated that "we were all Rwandans now and ethnic groups no longer mattered."

The museum is full of displays that try to explain the entire history of the conflict that arose from a differentiation of the Hutus and Tutsis, which was later capitalized on by politicians to push their own agendas in search of power. The people were conditioned to accept their roles in the slaughter and in the end over 800,000 were killed by machete, often neighbor against neighbor, and family members killing other family members.

The worst part of the museum for me was the rooms full of pictures of the people that had died in the killings. Half the second floor was dedicated to the kids that were lost, many often brutally slaughtered. I wish, as the museum states, that this should never happen again.

Bujumbura, Burundi. 6-7 February 2011

We flew into Bujumbura on Rwandan Air. We then spent a week in Burundi, first in the capital, Bujumbura, then driving around the countryside enjoying the beautiful scenery and friendly people. Our first experience was at a lakeside club watching American expats kite surfing. They said the risk of schistosomiasis was lower near the club but you had to watch out for the hippos.

It seems that most of the expats in Bujumbura hang out at the clubs on Lake Tanganyika and further inland muzungos weren't as common. The only ones we saw during our three days in the country worked for the international nongovernmental organizations CARE or Médecins sans Frontières (Doctors without Borders). There may have been more but usually we only saw the white faces in their SUVs emblazoned with their organizations stickers as they blew by us on the roads.

We visited the U.S. Embassy in Bujumbura and met with various offices who described their activities in Burundi. The embassy was concerned about crime, political violence, and terrorism and mentioned frequent attacks by "bandits" or the disenfranchised. The violence didn't target Americans but one did not want to get caught in the crossfire. Terrorism was a concern due to Burundi's involvement in Somalia under AMISOM and al-Shabaab had threatened to attack all countries that fought against them. As an AMISOM troop contributing country Burundi also received training under ACOTA however the U.S. had no little direct trade with Burundi.

Muzinda, Burundi. 8 February 2011.

As part of the work part of our visit to Burundi we drove out to a Burundian Army base and observed an explosive ordnance disposal (EOD) class taught by an American military team. The Americans were really there just to assist the Burundian instructor who taught simultaneously in French and in a local language. The instructor had gone to the U.S. for a course and was now being evaluated in how he presented the course material. There were twenty students in the three-week course but some of them were having problems with concepts that western students take for granted, like how there are satellites orbiting the earth that allow you to pinpoint your exact location. The students would immediately look up at the sky and try to spot the satellites and since they couldn't see them, wouldn't trust the GPS receiver.

Gitega, Burundi. 9 February 2011.

We drove out to the District Military Headquarters and met with its leadership. After a brief discussion, we toured the Commando Training School and watched commandos run through a high-flying obstacle course while carrying an 11kg (22 lb) rucksack. In between station the commandos would do pushups and sit-ups, then swing on ropes through the trees. The course and commandos were impressive and seemed enthusiastic about their training.

Several of the Commandos stayed with us the rest of the day as our guides and took us to the National Museum of Burundi. After tracking down the curator and waking him from his afternoon nap, he gave us a private tour of the museum that had many great artifacts carefully displayed. The section on musical instruments caught my eye and I was able to purchase a reproduction (non-artifact) Ikembe. An Ikembe is an instrument that has metal strips attached to a sounding box that is filled with metal shrapnel so that the box can be shaken to a beat and the strips twanged for sharper notes. There was also in the museum the head of a large hippo, a litter used to carry the king, an ancient man-made beehive, and an assortment of traditional weapons: spears, arrows, and bows.

We stopped at a great seminary in Gitega (Grand Seminary Jean Paul II) and the Abbot gave us a tour of his huge campus. There were over 40 buildings and it served as the largest seminary in the country. The seminary is self-sufficient and was adding new buildings to accommodate guests that come for conferences. I was impressed by the massive pigs being raised in the barn behind the seminary that weighed over three hundred pounds and were taller than Brad.

In both Rwanda and Burundi we saw many cattle and kids herding the cattle along the roads. Most of the sellers of charcoal along the roads in Burundi were kids as well, selling huge sacks of charcoal that were taller than they were. Many of the sacks were reused grain sacks with logos from USAID, a Turkish charity, or some other international aid organization.

We drove back to Bujumbura on improved dirt roads with great drainage and metal bridges with only the occasional delay caused by kids herding their cows along the road. In the mountain passes above Bujumbura, vehicles were stopped by tax collectors (our driver called them "bandits") for inspection. It seemed that every 500 meters someone had a sign on the ground by an 'official looking' pickup truck and they wanted to collect a different tax- charcoal, oil, banana beer, wood, etc., causing prices in Bujumbura to be twice the price of commodities in the countryside.

Bujumbura, Burundi. 10-11 February 2011.

During our trip we also visited a rock on a bluff overlooking a muddy brown river supposedly visited by Stanley and Livingston (as evidenced by their names and a date being carved into the rock) and the Olympic Center on the lake. Our driver said tourists liked to come see the rock (a large boulder over ten feet tall but he wasn't sure if it was really there that Stanley and Livingston visited. The Olympic center featured a soccer field and a building, but the building was closed. It didn't look like the field had been used in some time as some of the locals had started to plant corn along the outside of the field.

I enjoyed the many public service announcement billboard signs that were posted around the country. They were locally painted in French and warned people to use bed nets to stop malaria, breastfeed their babies, wash their hands, and watch out for men with money who will pay to have sex because then you'll get AIDS.

Burundi seemed like a nice country, however it was and still is facing many challenges. One comparatively minor problem was the government had sold, and then resold the frequency spectrum for the country causing the major communications countries to leave. Without a telecommunications company Burundi experienced very poor and sporadic Internet connectivity. Sometimes without warning the cell phones and land telephone network would stop working. The day I left the credit card and banks financial communication lines out of the country were disconnected so I could not get cash from the banks or use my credit card to pay my hotel bill. I ended up having to leave an IOU note and wiring the money when I returned to Dakar.

A major problem for the country are the many land disputes caused by returning refugees who retained their legal right to their abandoned lands, however the current occupants also had a legal right to the land. The court system is jammed up with cases like these where both claimants have a legal right to the land so some have taken to resolving the situation by lobbing grenades over walls in the middle of the night. I was told not to worry because the grenades and shootings weren't targeting muzungos.

Dakar, Senegal. 15 February 2011.

Back in Dakar I joined the U.S. Security Cooperation Office at the Embassy in its annual bilateral planning conference with the Senegalese military. In this meeting we reviewed the bilateral training over the past year and planned engagements for the upcoming three to five years: exercises, visiting training teams, courses for Senegalese officers in the states, and conference participation abroad. What was great about this conference is the Senegalese presented a clear picture of where they wanted to be a year later, knew what engagements they wanted, and provided frank, candid feedback on the past year's activities. The priorities for the Senegalese included peacekeeping and stability operations as well as counter-terrorism and border security. The comprehensive plan addressed all sectors of the military: medical, information technology, communications, EOD, Gendarmes, maritime, defense institution building, and even public affairs.

The Vermont National Guard was also a participant in the planning conference as they are the state partners for Senegal under the State Partnership Program (SPP). Under the SPP, ten African countries are partnered with state National Guard units establishing an ongoing habitual relationship. So when Senegal requests a mortar training team to visit and share a class on mortar employment, tactics, and procedures the state partner provides the team. This way the Senegalese and Vermont teams build a long-lasting relationship and partnership. The SPP usually branches out to be more than a military partnership as national guardsmen see opportunities to engage their new partners with other activities. For example, a key role of the National Guard is disaster response. Also Vermont is a major investor in solar energy, which is in high demand in Senegal. Other exchanges have been developed between the University of Vermont and the University in Dakar.

Dakar, Senegal. 22 February 2011.

Tasha and Brad flew into Dakar for the two-day Trans-Sahara Security Symposium in Dakar to assist as note takers and facilitators. Our job was to sit in the back of the room with the translators and take notes for the official record of the symposium and help out as needed.

The first presenter was retired Ambassador Fowler from Canada who was captured on 14 Dec 2008 and held hostage for 130 days. He was the UN special envoy to Niger and tried in this role to get the rebels and government to talk. Ambassador Fowler was invited to tour a Canadian uranium mine near the town of Karma, Niger when he was grabbed and driven north into the desert. At the conference he explained how they lived in the desert and described his captors as courageous, true believers who thought they had God's and the angel's protection. He thought it was evident his captors were not bandits but al Qaeda as they claimed.

Other presenters briefed on the security situation in Mali, the framework of ideology, tendencies and currents of contemporary Islam, and the growing threats of religious extremists. Presenters were university professors and general officers from the region and dialogue by the participants was extensive. All agreed action needed to be taken to combat regional security issues but there was some disagreement to the particulars.

9 MALI & UNREST IN DAKAR

Bamako, Mali. 9 March 2011.

I was surprised by the heat wave that hit me as I stepped off the plane at the Bamako airport. The past couple weeks have been windy and cool in Dakar and Bamako was a sharp contrast. The sky was white and I rarely saw blue above me in the six days we were in Mali. Natasha from Ethiopia joined me for this trip to Mali. I wanted to drive from Dakar to Bamako but the U.S. Embassy had recently published a travel warning for Mali due to fighting in the countryside and the threat of attacks or robberies from Touraeg or rebels.

As we drove through the city from the airport to our hotel I was struck by the number of people riding scooters and motorcycles. Dakar has some, but in Bamako there were swarms of scooters and they even had their own lanes in traffic. Everybody- men, women, and even some entire families on the same scooter were zipping around on the little scooters and it seemed that the other motorists took care to avoid them. The only accident I saw in Bamako was scooter against scooter where one was crushed on the road and the other was flung into a ditch 20 yards away. It must have been a recent accident because people were clustered near the bike in the ditch.

Another thing that stood out was the number of traffic lights in operation and that people actually respected them and waited for their turn to go. In Dakar working traffic lights were a novelty and most drivers simply drove when and where they wanted to.

Muammar Khadafi was still popular in Mali as he has been a major donor of a nearly completed new government office complex (named after himself). We drove by a sprawling new housing complex also built by Khadafi on the way to the hotel.

Our first visit in Mali was at the U.S. Embassy to Bamako where the American staff repeatedly emphasized the linkages between Mali and Libya. We were briefed on the complex political situation with coalitions, elections, and the threat from Tuareg rebels in the north. The biggest concern was security in the north and the security officer mentioned hostages held by AQIM. However, the Embassy was optimistic about upcoming elections and the peaceful transfer of power between governments.

While at the Embassy we were briefed on the security situation in the northern part of Mali and advised not to go to Dogon country as I had originally planned. The following day the US Embassy issued a Warden Message warning: "the Embassy has credible information of a possible attack in the immediate future against the U.S. Embassy in Bamako and U.S.-related interests to include the American International School of Bamako (AISB). It also has credible information of a possible kidnapping plot targeting Americans and other Westerners in Bamako."

Therefore I changed my plans to go south instead of north to Dogon or Timbuktu. I recently attended a conference where retired Canadian Ambassador Fowler spoke about his capture in December 2008 by AQIM and his subsequent captivity in the Sahel for five-months. I did not want to follow in his footsteps. I can always come back in the future and see the sights when things calm down.

In 2011 Bamako stood out for its democratically elected government and preparations for upcoming elections in 2012. Mali had seen the peaceful transfer of power from the military transitional government in 1992 (following a coup in 1991) to a democratically elected president and to another in 2002. In 2011 President Amadou Toumani Toure had promised to not run for a third 5-year term in 2012 and was reportedly clearing the way for a third democratically elected administration.

Mali's neighbors are also in election cycles with Liberia holding elections in October 2011 (President Sirleaf-Johnson had promised to serve only one term but is running again as she didn't see any other viable candidates) and in Senegal President Wade was running for a 3rd 5-year term in 2012. Mali is also being affected by refugees from neighboring Cote d'Ivoire where elections have failed to produce a functional government and the country is falling into civil war. Algeria and Mauritania are also experiencing ongoing demonstrations. It will be interesting to see how the region develops with its many conflicts.

Bamako, Mali. 10 March 2011.

Tasha and I traveled to the French Airbase in Bamako to observe U.S. funded contractors replace the engines on a Malian aircraft as part of a maintenance contract. It was interesting to tour a aircraft maintenance facility and see the American and Malian mechanics work together. The new engines had arrived and the old ones would be removed, crated, and shipped back to the states for an overhaul.

Later after lunch we visited the Mali Peacekeeping Center in Bamako where some U.S. instructors were presenting a course on information management in both French and English. The six-week course was made up of military professionals from Mali, Mauritania, Senegal, Burkina Faso, and Algeria.

Sikasso, Mali. 11 March 2011.

The drive from Bamako to Sikasso was nice for the most part and the roads were in pretty good condition until the end where Chinese/African road crews were working hard to pave a new section. I thought the 30min dirt road bypass was cool because it took us through several small villages and fields and we could see more (despite the thick dust) than just bushes along the road. Some of the construction vehicles were driving recklessly in the huge dust clouds and one plunged into a mud house near the side of the road, getting stuck completely inside. Luckily it didn't look like anyone was hurt.

Sikasso is the regional capital of the southernmost part of Mali and borders Cote d'Ivoire, Burkina Faso, and Guinea. It is also where many refugees from Cote d'Ivoire have been escaping into Mali. Between 2-3 million Malians reside in Cote d'Ivoire but since the recent conflict in Cote d'Ivoire many have been returning to Mali. However, as Malians in Mali they don't qualify for refugee aid since they are in their home country, instead they are simply known as internally displaced persons (IDP) and have to rely on the Malian government to take care of them.

In the evening we visited the Sikasso regional museum and received a guided tour from the museum director who explained a couple rituals of the secret societies and showed us some of the masks and weapons of the ancient hunters. The second part of the museum, and my favorite part, was dedicated to musical instruments from the region and had many on display including the Kora, Xylophone, Flutes, Tambours, and various forms of rattles and carved logs that made different sounds depending on how they were beaten.

Before leaving for Segou the following morning we visited a friend who offered to guide us around the city and show us Mamelon and the Tata. In the center of town near a market lies a hill that steeply rises 30 meters from the gently sloping plane and provides a commanding view of the area. The ancient inhabitants built a tower and series of tunnels to defend themselves from foreign invaders along with the Tata, a 4 to 6 meters high clay wall that surrounded the city. When invaders breeched the wall and fought their way to Mamelon the defenders would use the tunnels to surround them or escape and flank their attackers. The Tata wall served as a primary means of defense and originally featured rounded sections that provided over 200 degrees of visibility and ability to engage their enemies with poisoned arrows or rifles. The locals were able to use these defenses to successfully repel French colonial forces in the 1800s.

Segou, Mali. 12-13 March 2011.

After checking into our hotel in Segou the first thing we did was hire a guide to show us around. Unfortunately he told us it was too hot to go anywhere and he would be back in a couple hours to give us a tour. When he did come back at 4pm he took us to the Bogolan Workshop, where inside a classically decorated red mud building workers spun cotton string, wove it on looms, dyed, and stenciled fabric which they sold in the adjacent gallery. In order to make a finer quality fabric they cheated and mixed industrial string with the locally spun string, but the rest seemed legit and you could try your hand at smearing mud on a stencil to make designs.

As the sun began to set we drove out to village north of Segou to meet the chief and tour his village. The meeting began with our guide handing him 2500 CFA and then a kid walked in the door, saw me, yelled "toubab" and ran away screaming. The guide apologized because he said my white skin scared the kids. We next visited the chief's palace with seven meeting rooms made of red mud; one for each day of the week and Monday's room was the largest of all. On the outskirts of the village overlooking the Niger River was the oldest mosque in the region also made of mud with wooden beams protruding from the roof and tower. Our guide said it was so old they weren't sure who had built it or when it was built.

I loved exploring old mud villages and finding goats in a walled in courtyard or another old mosque with large ostrich eggs decorating the roof as ornaments. The village seemed deserted until we found a group of old men in white robes sitting under a large old tree near on the wide sandy banks of the river watching the pinkish-orange sunset.

Night fell as we drove back to the hotel and in the thick shadows hawkers tried to sell their trinkets or lure us over so they could pick our pockets. During dinner on the veranda others would throw their blankets, masks, or necklaces over the rail, hissing at us to take a look. If ignored they would hiss even louder or start to make comments like "what's the matter with you, you don't like black people?" or "hey, I'm talking to you! Its rude to ignore me!" Usually after a while they would go away, but in Segou they kept coming back, always interrupting a conversation to throw out a price "15,000 CFA (about $30) for the necklace" or some other obscene price.

The next morning the guide returned and we walked down to the river and took a motor-pirogue to a pottery village 7km upstream from Segou. The ride took an hour and we branched off the main Niger River into a channel that ended in thick lily pads and locals digging up mud and forming it into bricks. Some of the mud was carried back to the village where young girls mixed it with their feet and old ladies formed it into pottery. The men hauled large bushels of dried grass to a clearing in the center of town where the women arranged their pottery on the ground and set massive bonfires alight in order to bake the earthen vessels.

Back in Segou ladies sold the overpriced vases and plates on the banks of the river. I tried to negotiate, but the ladies insisted on fixed prices for tourists and I ended up leaving empty handed.

Dakar, Senegal. 19 March 2011.

Today, 19 March 2011, is the date set by opposition groups and protesters to gather together and voice their unhappiness about increasing food prices, insufficient power and frequent power outages, and to protest President Wade's decision to run for a third term. The date is significant as 19 March is the 11th anniversary of President Wade's presidency. Twenty-four permits to demonstrate were filed and despite being initially denied, all were eventually approved.

Crowd control vehicles with water cannons moved into town last night and early this morning riot police entered the Place d'Independance and set up barricades. As demonstrators gathered to the Place d'Independance the police stood calmly in formation holding batons and resting their shields on the ground. Some police even lounged on crates of teargas in the shade under the trees. By noon a couple thousand people had gathered to the square and vendors were making their rounds selling belts, watches, peanuts, and even balloons. Down the road a group was handing out small Senegalese flags and the demonstration seemed to have more of a carnival like atmosphere than a serious uprising staged to overthrow the government.

Around 12:30 the crowd become more agitated and some surged to the barricades nearest the riot police and started tearing up posters of President Wade and throwing them at the police. Shortly after that I heard the low thump of teargas canisters being shot into the air and the crowd split with about half running across the Place. The barricades quickly disappeared and the riot police moved from a line formation to a square "phalanx" formation but still held back away from the crowd. Some of the protestors came back and started to set banners and signs on fire and the riot police formations started to move forward. The smoke from the fire grew so the lead riot police platoons started to run forward with the water cannon truck closely behind and the crowd scattered. By 1pm the Place d'Independence was mostly empty besides riot police and onlookers so traffic began to circulate again. I did not see anyone get hurt or even the riot police get near the protestors.

Up the hill from the Place d'Independence outside the Presidential Palace a Pro-Wade demonstration was being set up with a reviewing tent full of chairs, colorful banners, and posters.

This morning the opposition had its turn to demonstrate, which ended by being dispersed by Riot Police firing teargas, and this afternoon the Pro-Wade or "Wadists" had their opportunity to demonstrate their support of President Wade. Thousands made their way to the Presidential Palace carrying signs and banners and accompanied by drummers and sound trucks. It seemed the Wadists greatly outnumbered the opposition demonstrators from this morning.

Around 4:30pm the first wave of the long pro-Wade parade arrived at the gates of the Presidential Palace after marching down the corniche and through the downtown "Plateau" neighborhood. People continued to stream into the square in front of the Presidential Palace for over an hour until the streets around the intersection were packed in every direction. Riot police tried to control the crowd, which was generally peaceful with supporters wearing a variety of Pro-Wade T-Shirts and waving blue flags. I decided to leave the square when the people around me started to get knocked down by the pressing crowd. Riot police also formed a line on the road to Place d'Independance and seemed ready to face any threat coming from where the morning Anti-Wade protests took place. The Place d'Independance was now empty besides a few lonely cabs driving around in circles.

As I walked home I noticed several empty buses parked on the side streets adorned or painted with the names of outlying villages. One of my Senegalese friends later told me that the Wadists had paid people in the villages to get on the government funded buses and come to the city to demonstrate in favor of President Wade. The protesters were locals who had arrived spontaneously but the pro-Wade rally had been organized and paid for by the government.

10 DRC & CONGO

Kinshasa, DRC. 3-6 April 2011.

Sunday afternoon I caught the plane from Dakar to Kinshasa via Nairobi, a flight that has become routine for me. Monday afternoon I arrived in the capital of the Democratic Republic of Congo and made my way to Jason's apartment in Kinshasa. Jason climbed Kilimanjaro with me earlier in the year and now hosted a small group of us for our visit to the Congos. Shortly after arriving at my friends house the rain that surprised me in Nairobi found me again soaking the Congolese capital.

Unfortunately at the same time the storm hit, a UN flight from eastern DRC was attempting to land and was caught up in a wind shear which smashed the small plane into the ground, killing all but one passenger. We later learned that the pilots of the crashed UN flight were from a former Soviet republic and the pilots were drunk and refused the towers instructions to not land but circle around again.

At the time another friend, Brian, was stuck circling above in a SAA flight that only revealed to its passengers that there was a delay due to the weather conditions. When he landed 30 minutes later he said he had no idea that there had been a recent accident and saw several wrecks on the ground around the airfield.

When we were all together on ground at Jason's apartment he gave us the low down on life in Kinshasa: even though crime is considered critically high there haven't been any violent acts against expats. You had better lock your car doors as people will try to open them in traffic or when you slow down for the many potholes or even larger road craters. He also said only crazy people take taxis in Kinshasa as many have been driven off and robbed at gunpoint. A recent scam was for locals to approach an expat and flash a badge and say they were undercover police, then pull a gun and force the victim into a vehicle. However, he said the robbers are usually polite and have been known to leave enough money to catch a cab back to where they were abducted. My friend also warned me not to take any photos of anything or anybody as until recently photography was against the law and police continued to seize cameras from tourists. Armed with this knowledge we stayed in for dinner that night.

On Tuesday, my second day in Kinshasa we attempted to visit the Bonobo monkey reserve outside of town but Jason got lost. To our surprise we ended up a couple hours later making a giant circle around the town to his neighborhood again. We gave up, got some lunch, and headed to the Bralima Brewery, a place he easily found.

There wasn't much for expats to do in Kinshasa so Jason had toured it several times. He arranged an official tour guide who took us through the museum of old vats and then through the soda section (Coke, Fanta, and Schweppes) and into the much larger beer section. At the end of the tour we were escorted to a beer garden and offered as much as we could drink of whatever we wanted. My friends started with the Turbo King (7% alcohol rumored to be mixed with nicotine), and then moved on to the more traditional Primus and Legend beers while I sampled the Fanta, Sprite, and Soda water. After the heat of the day we crashed for a while in my friends air-conditioned apartment before going out for dinner at the British High Commission.

The expat community in Kinshasa is very small and often Embassies host themed nights and we were lucky enough to be there for pub quiz night. Dinner was brochettes and rice but everyone was there for the quiz game and tables worked together to answer the trivia questions. We didn't win but it was good to spend time with the Brits and other expats. We left just before the rain started and I soon fell asleep to the sound of a steady rain on the pavement below.

Pointe Noire, Republic of Congo. 7 April 2011.

It rained all night and even though it slackened in the morning a constant drizzle accompanied us as our 4x4 waded axle deep through the streets of Kinshasa. At the port we discovered that piles of debris washed downstream by the heavy rains had trapped our speedboats in their berths. After much searching, we found a middleman who arranged a crossing for us for $250 on a smaller boat with a braver pilot. It took about 15 minutes to cross the wide muddy waters as the pilot deftly guided us around floating islands of logs and bushes to the Republic of Congo.

On the shore we were met by soldiers and customs officials who guarded us until our passports were stamped and we were allowed to enter the much cleaner and relaxed of the two Congos. In Brazzaville, the capital of the Republic of Congo, the streets were cleaner, traffic flowed better and overall it was less chaotic. It was as if the palpable veil of tension in Kinshasa had been lifted and we could breathe easier.

We didn't spend too much time exploring the city before we headed to the airport to catch a Trans Air Congo (TAC) flight to Pointe Noire. We boarded the plane on time, but then the flight sat on the tarmac for an hour as we waited for thunderstorms passing through the area to clear. It was an old plane, but packed to the rafters with people and bags in a first come, first served seating arrangement that resulted in a mad scramble to load first and get the best seats. Fortunately an hour after lifting off we landed in Pointe Noire on the Atlantic coast of Congo.

The worst part of the flight was retrieving our bags in the Pointe Noire terminal. The workers pushed the full luggage carts up to an opening in the wall and shoved the bags through. The crowd of passengers jammed into the narrow space and fought for their luggage. Bags at the top of the cart that weren't immediately claimed were knocked off the cart and formed a pile that passengers climbed over to reach their own bags. We decided to stand off a bit and let the crowd settle before fighting to retrieve our luggage. Finally, about 40 minutes later we were able to make our way to the cart and get our bags.

We checked into the swank Atlantic Palace Hotel in the center of downtown, situated on the main strip between the posh offices of the oil magnates of ENI and Total. Pointe Noire is a resort and oil town with a large expat and tourist population with direct flights from Europe that bypass the Congolese capital cities. The first place we headed after the hotel was La Pyramide, a surf restaurant/club that played Jack Johnson from a tiki bar that overlooked a decent beach break. Unfortunately the dude that took care of the surfboards couldn't be found so I couldn't get wet.

Pointe Noire, Republic of Congo. 8 April 2011.

The next morning I ran along the coast and the waves were still knee to waist high but the board rental dude was still missing. I couldn't find any other places that rented surfboards so I ran along the sandy roads for an hour before heading back to the hotel and getting ready for work.

We went to the Port Autonome de Pointe Noire to meet the Belgian Navy Ship Godesia, which was arriving as part of the African Partnership Station (APS) program. APS is an AFRICOM program with international partners to enhance maritime security. For this event participants from Congo, Gabon, and Benin had been afloat for two months on the Belgian ship working with naval forces from the region on interdiction on sea, boarding procedures, interactions with law enforcement.

In the port we watched a Belgian Navy Ship attempt to dock at the pier but it smashed a container ship berthed nearby on its approach. Eventually the Belgians got their ship parked and a Congolese Navy band and a ceremonial platoon of Soldiers carrying rifles and wearing red pompoms on their berets met them.

We had traveled to Pointe Noire with a U.S. Navy lawyer who presented classes on the role of the Commander in disciplined military operations, African charter on human and people's rights as well as the use of force in military law enforcement and security duties. The class paid close attention and asked situational questions that showed they understood the legal concepts and how they should be applied at sea.

We ate lunch onboard with the senior officers and toured the ship before heading back to the hotel. In the evening I headed back to la Pyramide and the board dude was there but there were no waves! In the end we ended up hanging out with a Lufthansa aircrew and bodysurfing in the weak crumbly waves.

Pointe Noire, Republic of Congo. 9-10 April 2011.

On our final day in Pointe Noire a morning surf check revealed no more waves. It had gone completely flat. The airport and flight back on Trans Air Congo provided the fun for the day. 300 people packed the tiny airport, each one in line practically with their arms around the person in front of them to stop people from cutting in line. If you left three inches of space between you and the person in front of you at least one person would try to slip into the gap. By the time I finished checking the bags and getting our tickets my clothes were soaked with sweat. I had to guzzle a 1.5 liter bottle of water to rehydrate.

About 30 minutes later the flight boarded and surprisingly we departed on time and soon we were back on the ground in Brazzaville. Trans Air Congo, lovingly known as TAC, is my least favorite of all African Airlines thanks to the fight to get a seat (aka open seating), limited service (a tiny 2oz cup of Coke or Fanta for the inflight service), crumbling plane (broken filthy seats, nonfunctional seat belts), and bouncing one-wheeled landings.

On the ground (the passengers broke into applause after surviving the landing) we had to go through customs and passport control even though it was a domestic flight since we were non-Africans before we could get to the mele of baggage claim. Finally with our bags collected we made our way through the deserted streets of downtown Brazzaville to the Adonis Hotel for the night. I was surprised at how quiet the city was on the weekend and we wandered around without being hassled by any vendors or beggars. We visited the de Braza museum/mausoleum, which celebrates the life of the Pierre de Braza who negotiated the treaty for the creation of the Republic of Congo and spent a good portion of his life exploring the territory that he claimed for France. In the basement of the marble walled building Pierre de Braza is entombed with his family. I recommend staying away from the walls if you visit as two marble plates fell off the wall and nearly brained one of my two traveling companions. The museum director came running down the stairs when he heard the crash and was relieved to see no one was hurt. He tried to calm us by saying that "these things happen from time to time" and quickly went about replacing the thick panels.

We ate dinner at a restaurant overlooking the Congo River and watched the lights across the way in Kinshasa. From a distance the city was nice and I was impressed to see the power stayed on through dinner. After dinner I returned to the hotel while my traveling companions went to the Boom Boom and No Stress clubs to check out the local scenery.

The next morning we packed up our bags and made our way to the port for the boat ride back to Kinshasa. This time the speedboat crossed the wide brown river in three minutes but clearing customs on both sides took ten times longer on each side.

Kisangani, DRC. 12 April 2011.

It seems like it rains every time I get on a plane in the DRC. This morning when we set out for the airport at 0500 the roads were already a good foot deep in water and in a couple places the roads had a current and rapids marked the potholes in the street. One of my friends scored seats on a MONUSCO flight so we were flying for free to Kisangani. The line was chaotic to register for the flight and the babel from the UN workers gave way to English as the universal language to share information. They tried to enforce order on the line but gave up and handled the check-in like in any other African airport as the crowd pressed to the front. A couple flights were scheduled for the morning but one was canceled due to the weather and most were delayed several hours, including ours to Kisangani. The flight was only a third full and we had plenty of space to stretch out on the Boeing 737-200 for the three-hour flight (drink service by the Spanish UN crew included).

On the ground in Kisangani we were met by an American western cowboy wearing a white five-gallon hat who drove us into town and past the agricultural project and fish ponds he was managing for Texas A&M. After checking into our hotel we set out to explore the town and ended up eating stewed goat over rice in a local restaurant then visiting the Greek Cultural Center. For fun later we took moto-taxis across town and hung out with some other locals. UN and many other lettered vehicles were constantly circulating through town but most of the Bangladeshi and Uruguayan blue hats were restricted to their bases and not able visit town like us. It seemed pretty safe there, much nicer than Kinshasa, so it seemed odd that the UN troops thought they needed to stay cloistered behind concertina wire, high walls, and machine guns in guard posts.

Kisangani, DRC. 13 April 2011.

It's the rainy season in the parts of DRC that are south of the equator and thankfully the temperatures are lower when it rains. Wednesday started off cool with light showers as we toured the fish farm and agricultural project operated by Texas A&M. The project was designed to feed a nearby Congolese military base of approximately 800 to 1000 Soldiers and allow them to be self-sufficient. 43 fishponds are located on and around the base and many are linked together through a gravity fed system that contains about 40,000 tilapia and African catfish. The fishponds provide 800 fish (400 kg) per week and the surrounding hills were developed as farm project fields of rice, cassava, and a variety of vegetables. Unfortunately the contract for the project was set to expire in September and the project managers haven't heard if the contract will be renewed.

The project manager chose fish as his protein source in designing the project as it is easier to sustain and harder to steal when the project is terminated. He said cattle are easy to steal and relocate, but fishponds will continue to reproduce, as it's hard to catch all the fish. He expected the ponds to be productive for the next ten years without any intervention but restocking and adding nutrients and vitamins would help maintain the genetic pool.

In the afternoon we visited the market in Kisangani and got hassled by people yelling "Muzungo!" and "Mondele!" (roughly translated as "white guys") and others calling after us "tiki tiki tiki" (no translation but they would say it after we walked by without buying anything). The massive dense market sprawled for a couple blocks and had everything- there was a car part section, bicycle section, food, clothing, furniture, luggage and so on, sold from little wooden stalls roughly two meters wide and with a broken one meter wide path between booths.

Later we ended up hanging out at the Texas A&M house with their crew, a couple UN officials, and some locals for a good old Texas barbecue. Power kept dropping though out the night and eventually we found some candles (a general lack of fuel in the region negated running the generator) to eat by candlelight. One old Congo hand asked, "What did they use for light in the Congo before candles?" The answer: "electricity."

Kisangani, DRC. 14 April 2011.

Most of my crew was worn out after a late night at the Texas A&M house and cruising a couple bars until the early hours of the morning so we took it easy. We toured the UN logistics base on the river, then drove downstream and ate lunch at a restaurant in a bamboo forest overlooking the river. The food was outstanding, with fresh beef imported from South Africa, and monkeys in the trees provided the entertainment.

On the way to the restaurant by the river we passed several large plantations with impressive mansions that stretched to the water. Our local guide remarked that the people who owned the restaurant where we ate had owned a previous site closer to town along the river. Unfortunately when government officials saw how nice their place was they seized it for themselves and the former owners had to relocate further away from town.

The main event for the day was a soccer match featuring the local military team against a civilian team from another city. Since it was a Thursday afternoon the crowds were light but there were lots of armed

Soldiers and police to keep order. The visitors won with the only score of the match but whenever the crowd got rowdy security would beat them with long sticks from their position on the walls.

After dinner, groups of vendors tracked us down at our hotel to sell us all kinds of tourist trinkets: swagger sticks, carved monkeys, masks, paintings, and so on. Surprisingly they knew where we were staying and that we were leaving in the morning. But in our three days here we had seen less than a dozen other muzungos so I reckon we weren't that hard to find.

Kinshasa, DRC. 15 April 2011.

The morning began with a sob story from the T-Shirt guy. My friend who was showing us around Kisangani has a guy who makes custom t-shirts with whatever my friend wants written on them for $15 each. Last night the T-Shirt guy delivered the t-shirts and had a friend along with him who sold a couple masks and other trinkets. Turns out the friend took all the money from the shirts after they left and the following morning the T-Shirt guy was back demanding to be paid again.

Next up demanding money was the car rental guy who asked for an extra days car rental since he was driving us to the airport, plus $100 for gas money, even though the truck was delivered on empty. The demands for extra money began as it was time to leave for the airport and they refused to move until we paid, making us late for our flight.

Once we were done negotiating we started on our way to the airport and ran into a local military friend who went to the soccer game with us the previous day. He offered to come with us in case we ran into any problems, and he was key in getting us onto the UN airport for our flight home.

A roadblock was set up outside the airport and security was refusing to allow entry without payment and cars were backed up at least a quarter mile. The private security and heavily armed military guarding the base and pushing mob yelling in Swahili and Lingala at the gate reminded me of movies I had seen of people cut off just out of the reach of safety. I was very glad when our new friend parted the intense crowd for us and got us on the base.

It was great to get another free UN flight, but this time instead of a Spanish flown 737-200 we got the chance to fly on an old Russian Antonov-24 twin turboprop airplane. The Antonov-24 was first introduced in 1959 and this plane looked like it was an original model that had passed through many years of hard service. I was relieved when the cramped rusty old plane rolled to a stop in Kinshasa four hours later, especially when I saw the bald tires had worn through a layer of strings. At least the flight was free.

Kinshasa, DRC. 16 April 2011.

The highlight of the day: Bonobos! We woke up early and fought traffic for nearly two hours to Lola ya bonobo at the Petites Chutes de la Lukaya. Jason had received better driving directions and we finally made it to the site. The waterfall is located on a rutted 4x4 track in the hills outside of Kinshasa and is home to scores of Bonobos, small monkeys very similar to chimpanzees. Most of the Bonobos were rescued from hunters or markets and now spend their time wandering around their large fenced enclosures chucking mud at the curators and following around tourists. There is also a separate enclosure complete with human surrogate mothers for the baby Bonobos.

We saw at least two dozen Bonobos of all ages as we took the guided tour around the compounds. It was interesting to watch them as they walked along the fence with us. When we reached the end of a compound they would scream and another group of monkeys would run out of the bush and meet the group at the start of the next fence and keep us company. Park entry was only $5 USD, cheaper than parking (with the mandatory car wash). After the tour we had a tasty but overpriced lunch ($34 USD each) next to the waterfall and watched some tourists frolic in the dirty brown water.

Getting back to Kinshasa traffic was hell. We got caught on a narrow market street with trucks parked facing both directions on both sides of the road, severely restricting vehicular flow. Worse for us was that we were stuck surrounded by irate Congolese who targeted us for their anger. We were stopped behind four other cars and had several more behind us, but our car was soon encircled by people banging on our car and telling us to back up or get out of the way, but we couldn't move. We tried to tell them the cars around us had to move so we could move, but they only got angrier and started pounding on the windshield. Eventually (15 minutes later) a driver returned to the car that was blocking the way ahead of us and traffic started to move again. The mob got back in their cars and trucks and started driving as well, much to our relief.

Ever the glutton for punishment we drove straight to a tourist market where we were immediately surrounded again by vendors pushing bracelets, necklaces, carved items, and other junk while my friend tried to negotiate a reasonable price for a Tintin in Congo painting. The vendor refused to go below $15 each and we ended up walking away empty handed but severely harassed. Later we had some antelope and ostrich as a farewell dinner and prepared to leave DRC.

Nairobi-Johannesburg-Dakar. 17-19 April 2011.

Getting home to Dakar took me on a tour of Africa. Getting out of the Kinshasa airport wasn't that bad. Our checked bags were hand searched at two different points, I was wanded a couple times, and we spent a couple hours sweating while waiting for the plane. Luckily I got to Nairobi without any problem and the shuttle from the Tribe hotel was waiting for me. I agree with the website "Stuff Expat Aid Workers like" it's a relief to see someone holding a sign with your name on it when you fly into an airport.

The Tribe hotel was luxurious- nice people, beautiful hotel, and great food. The room was fantastic- it even had an electric hot water kettle. Of the three hotels I have used in Nairobi (I also stayed at the Hilton and Windsor), in my opinion the Tribe is the best. Just take a cab for $20 instead of the $40 airport shuttle.

The next morning when I returned to the airport in Nairobi to catch my flight to Dakar I was surprised to get a confused look from the check-in agent. He said my flight was cancelled last week (I should have checked the flight status so it was my fault, according to him) and the next flight was in two days. Luckily the sales office was able to get me on a flight back to Dakar thru Johannesburg on South African Airlines. So I flew Kenya Airways to Jo'burg, waited for five hours, and then caught an eight-hour flight on SAA to Dakar, arriving around 1am. At least I got lots of airline miles. I should be able to get a free flight to Hawaii after all this travel in Africa.

☐

11 SENEGAL & THE GAMBIA

Sali Portugal, Senegal. 24 April 2011.

One of my favorite things about Senegal is that the country observes both Muslim and Christian holidays. My Senegalese Christian friend from Joal invited a visiting friend and myself over for a family Easter celebration with dozens of kids and great food. I enjoyed talking to the elders and learning about his dad's career in the Senegalese Navy and visiting Europe. Afterwards we walked over to Leopoldo Senghor's (the first President of Senegal) house and got a private tour of the place where he was raised. The guide had lots of interesting stories like how Senghor's dad prophesied his rise to international fame when he first saw his mom (he told his buddy that even though she was ugly she would bear him a son who would take his name to all the world).

Later that evening we toured the seashell island of Fadiouth and my Senegalese friend dispelled all the untruths that my previous guide had told me. For example, the large baobab in the center of the island was not used as a human sacrificial alter. Be careful of your guides, many are just telling stories they think tourists want to hear. As we climbed the dirty-white seashell cemetery the sun set over the mangroves and the golden light reflected in the puddles as the tide went out. Loud music played in the background as the crowds on the shore swayed to the beat of the tambour. We drove back to our hotel in Saly in the dark, dodging cows and people on the pitch-black road.

Réserve de Bandia, Senegal. 25 April 2011.

The Réserve de Bandia is only 18km north of Saly so the next morning we headed north in my LandCruiser for a mini-Safari. At the park we paid 10,000 CFA each, 10,000 CFA for my truck, and 4,000 CFA for a guide to show us around the park. Surprisingly this was my first "Safari" in Africa even though I had already visited 17 African countries and traveled thousands of miles back and forth across the continent. This was a low budget and quick Safari, but not bad.

The only carnivores in the Park are a couple hyenas kept in a zoo-like enclosure and the well-fed crocodiles in the pond next to the reception area and restaurant. Driving around for our two hour safari we saw about a dozen giraffes of all sizes, scores of monkeys, at least a hundred antelope-cheval, 15-20 warthogs, 10 or so zebras, herds of water buffalos, flocks of ostriches, and two white rhinos. We stayed in the car for the most part except when the guide told us to get out 20ft from the female rhino to take a picture. She told us to be very quiet and not make any sudden movements, but remained in the car to take the picture.

The other place where we dismounted the trusty Landcruiser was at a giant Baobab tree in the middle of the park. Legend has it that the bodies of deceased Griots (local spiritual leaders) were interred in the openings of the giant Baobab trees until forbidden by President Senghor in the 1960s. The ban on the traditional practice that had taken place for as long as the people could remember caused a great drought that lasted six years and was only appeased when the massive tree was fed again. The Baobab tree in the park still has human skulls and bones visible in its dark hollows.

We ate lunch on an old McDonalds plastic picnic table and watched the monkeys steal bread from children. Sneaky crocodiles would try to get close to the monkeys as they pretended to bask in the sun and giant iguanas or Komodo dragons roamed the pathways near the bathrooms.

For the price and proximity to Dakar I would recommend the Bandia for those on a quick visit to Senegal. Niokolo Koba National Park, located another five hours east of Bandia, offers a much larger park and features a couple lions. However there isn't much in the way of large animals left in Senegal or West Africa as the locals already ate them. Most of the animals at Bandia and Niokolo Koba are imports from other parks on the continent.

Dunes at Lompoul, 5 May 2011.

Senegal lies on the edge of the Sahel desert and in Lompoul one can have the true desert experience by trekking through the dunes on camels, getting your Landcruiser stuck in the deep orange sand, and sleeping in tents. We met our guide at Lompoul village who directed me along sandy paths out into the open desert. Three kilometers from the village the dirt trail turned into sand, which quickly deepened as you entered the sand dunes. I soon had to shift into 4-Low but eventually the truck was stuck, axle deep in the sand. Luckily the guide figured out what I did wrong and after letting almost all the air out of the tires I was able to float/crawl the rest of the way to the camp.

There are a couple companies offering a camping in the sand dunes experience and we stayed with Lodge Senegal upon the recommendation of friends and it was an enjoyable experience (besides no bed nets to keep the mosquitoes away). We lounged on giant pillows and goatskins in the central tent before taking a couple camels across the dunes at sunset.

At dinner we found ourselves surrounded by Italians, French, and Spaniards and enjoyed a local meal of Senegalese couscous, a red stew with vegetables, and fried chicken. This place was totally off the grid and the only light was by lantern. However each tent had a private bathroom with a shower, flushing toilet, and sink with running water. We paid the resident rate at 35,000 CFA ($70 USD) each and the camel rides were only 3,500 CFA ($7 USD) each!

The next morning we headed to Saint Louis and I had the thrill of bombing down the dunes and through the deep sand back to the village and road. At the "service station" next to the mosque in town a local refilled my tires and blew out my air filter for a moderate charge and we were back on the road. If you follow the road to the ocean you can visit Lompoul by the Sea, which is a small fishing village with a large fish drying area on the beach.

Banjul, Gambia. 8 May 2011.

This morning a couple friends and I piled into my Landcruiser and headed south to the Gambia. Sunday morning is the best time to leave Dakar as there was no traffic and we made it to Mbour within an hour. As we drove further away from Dakar the roads steadily got worse, and after Kaolack we were swerving all over the road to avoid the craters that could swallow whole one of the omnipresent decrepit yellow taxis. After a while we gave up on the semi-paved road and traveled on the dirt track beside the road with everyone else.

The border crossing into the Gambia was nothing spectacular.

We stopped at the police station where they wrote our info into an old ledger, stamped our passports, then we drove around the barrier into the Gambia. In the Gambia the immigration officials seemed surprised to see us and used their cell phone to call for advice from their boss. Thirty minutes later they stamped our passports and we were on our way again.

At least the Gambians didn't pretend to pave their roads and their wide dirt highway was much easier on the bones. Within 20 minutes we were at the river ferry crossing (after being held up by an armed Gambian Soldier asking for money to buy a cold soda). The booth to buy tickets to cross the river on the boat was at the edge of town, which we had missed and discovered once we were in line. Thankfully, as the boat was about to load, they sold us a $4 ticket and we drove right onto the ferry. We were joined by a number of car rapides (small van-like buses), taxis, sept-places (seven passenger station wagons that carry people as long distance taxis), and pedestrians for the quick 15 min ride across the river. As usual in Africa anywhere there are people and cars we were swarmed by vendors selling cold drinks, cookies, underwear, and anything else you could imagine.

Once on the southern bank of the river we continued on a dirt road and raced west across the countryside to Banjul. It seemed that every 15 minutes or so we encountered a police or military checkpoint where we would be questioned about who we were, where we were from, where we were going, and why. Eventually a supervisor would wave us through and we would be off again. About 50km east of Banjul we ran into a Chinese road paving crew hard at work. They were improving the dirt road by covering it with a couple more inches of dirt, then rolled over with a steam roller to smooth it out, oiled the new dirt surface, and capped it with a couple inches of asphalt. The resulting road was smooth and shiny, but I wonder how long it will last.

In Banjul a very rare and surprising sight in Africa stopped us: a working stoplight that was respected by traffic! I sat in shock behind other cars halted by a red light with no crossing traffic and no police in sight. It was a nice welcome to Banjul and soon we arrived at our fancy hotel on the beach. The entire trip took 9 hours from Dakar to Banjul including the ferry ride, border crossing, road construction, and multiple checkpoints in the Gambia.

Banjul, Gambia. 9 May 2011.

Gambia is a major European tourist destination and has incredible hotels and restaurants besides the usual tourist markets. Banjul distinguishes itself, however, by specializing in sex tourism trade for older European women. Older white women are frequently seen in the company of young local Gambian men who ensure that their needs are taken care of and serve as their guides. Now is the low tourist season so there aren't that many people around, but during the high season busloads of tourists who fly direct from Europe are deposited on the tourist strip by the Senegambia hotel. This is also where most of the pickpockets work, but fortunately violent crime is very rare here.

Banjul, Gambia. 10 May 2011.

Today we hired a boat to show us the most dominant feature in the country, the Gambia River. First we rocketed out into the open sea to troll for barracuda in the dual engine speedboat, bouncing over waves so high that the propellers were out of the water. Then we motored up the river for 45 minutes to Juffare, a village on the river where Alex Haley traced his 'Roots'. There isn't much to the village, besides a small museum that talks about slavery and the ruins of a couple old buildings (chapel and storehouse). There is also the Kinte family house with some relatives but they weren't around the day we visited.

After the village we followed the route of the captured slaves to James Island, a former British fort where slaves were held for transport to Goree Island in Dakar, and then on to the new world. The island is slowly eroding into the river and all that remains are a few crumbling walls and large baobab trees.

On our way back to Banjul we stopped and tried our luck fishing first off Dog Island, then a couple other places but only caught 1 small (10 inch) silvery fish. At the end our boat captain took us on a shortcut slaloming through the mangroves to another spot where we caught a red snapper and a trout.

Banjul, Gambia. 11 May 2011.

One of my friends that came down on this trip to the Gambia and Guinea-Bissau works in HIV Education and Prevention so as part of this trip we got to watch some of the training she sponsored and coordinated in the Gambia. The instructors were doctors who gave a detailed presentation on how HIV is transmitted, showed graphic pictures, gave a demonstration on how to use male and female condoms (using fruit), talked about stigma, and answered questions from the group. Most of the speakers were male, but the female speaker they affectionately called "Aunty" stole the show.

There were only three females in the crowd of about 65 people who attended the class and Aunty directed some of her comments to the women, like don't fall for sexual harassment for a promotion because most likely they don't have the power to promote you if you have sex with them. However, Auntie's greatest role was to give a wife's perspective on HIV and AIDS. Aunty spoke to them in the local language so I didn't understand much but the crowd continuously roared with laughter. I thought her perspective was interesting as many men in the Gambia have more than one wife.

The Gambian doctors boiled HIV prevention down to the A, B, Cs:

A- Abstain. This caused a lot of chatter in the local language, but some devout Muslims were being cheerfully poked by their friends for abstaining by reason of their religion and they had never touched a woman. They were a very small part of the group.

B- Be Faithful. Don't cheat and if you have more than one wife, don't stray outside of your family.

C- Condoms. Condoms cost less than 10 Dalasis each (approx. $0.36 USD) and many free condoms were available at the meeting and other hospitals and clinics around the city.

After the meeting the participants walked to the nearby clinic where they got a free lunch and a t-shirt for participating. Then the participants went through pre-testing counseling, drew blood for testing, and then went through post-testing counseling where a doctor or nurse privately discussed the results. Estimates of the prevalence of HIV/AIDS vary but the CIA Factbook estimates a 2% prevalence rate in the Gambia.

At dinner I was introduced to a scientist who was conducting HIV research in the Gambia with the British Medical Research Council (MRC) looking for a link between HIV-II and HIV-I. According to the researcher HIV-II patients survive much longer than those with HIV-I although it is possible to have both at the same time. The hope is to find a way to help HIV-I patients live longer by learning from HIV-II. The MRC is conducting a longitudinal study with local infected patients and is hopeful although concerned that funding is decreasing.

Banjul, Gambia. 12-13 May 2011.

Today we started the drive back to Dakar but decided to drive back around the Gambia through the Casamance region. After a short two hour drive we arrived at the southern border of the Gambia and met a pre-arranged military escort to get through the Casamance. The region is known for its amazing beaches but inland also for its ongoing insurgency where Senegalese troops have been ambushed by rebels by a group demanding its independence from Senegal. Our military escort consisted of two gun trucks with heavy caliber machineguns mounted in the truck bed with a squad of eight heavily armed troops in each truck. At the outposts by the borders I also spotted a Senegalese wheeled tank with a 100mm main gun. Our trip through the combat zone took about four hours as we had to travel at the speed of our escorts but passed without any incidents. Once we were through the Casamance we waved goodbye to our escort and continued on our way to Tambacounda in the far south-east corner of Senegal near the border with Burkina Faso.

As we were speeding along the road in southern Senegal we were surprised to see a white girl sitting under a tree along the side of the road outside a very small village so I slammed on the breaks and reversed back to the girl. Turns out she was a Peace Corps Volunteer who was waiting for a ride to Tambacounda but none of the sept-places taxis had any room for her. She was supposed to spend the night at the Peace Corps house there and then continue on to Dakar for a meeting at the Headquarters the next day. She was tiny and famished and devoured the three king-sized snickers bars I had in my backpack. She said she had run out of protein powder several months ago and was subsisting on a cup of rice a day (she claimed to have lost 30 lbs). She received a $300 per month allowance from the Peace Corps but someone in her "family" had been stealing it little by little. She lived in a one-room hut without a door among a cluster of huts that belonged to the family. Her job was to work on environmental projects at the local school.

After dropping her off at the Peace Corps house, we checked into the hotel and explored Tambacounda. There wasn't much to the town, which consisted mainly of dirt roads, mosques, tailor shops, carpenters, and welders. However, we found attached to a large Catholic church the Dom Bosco Trade School with a mechanic garage that taught trade skills.

The next day we picked up our Peace Corps friend and drove back to Dakar north of the Gambia. The drive took six hours as the road was in bad shape with giant potholes east of Kaolack. Our new friend enjoyed the air conditioned ride in the comfortable Landcruiser and told us stories of lions in the Nikolo Koba Park near Kaolack and Peace Corps life on the border with Burkina Faso.

She said the region grew lots of rice and peanuts and that Senegalese President Wade got all the votes from the village after he donated a millet grinder before the last election. She also spoke of farmers smoking a lot of weed brought in from the Gambia twice a week by bicycle and that marijuana use was the reason why nothing gets accomplished. She said the village doctor was usually high or drunk, as were most of the men in the village. This was the reason she and her "family" were malnourished and survived on a cup of rice per person each day. Another village nearby was made up of cotton sharecroppers where the cotton company provided the seed, fertilizer, and tools and the villagers got to keep 10% of the harvest.

12 ETHIOPIA, CHAD, & CAMEROON

Addis Ababa, Ethiopia. 17-18 May 2011.

I am running out of travel money so I am economizing by taking the cheapest flights possible. Unfortunately the cheapest flights also involve some long out of the way routes and layovers. For example, I left Dakar on Tuesday afternoon and got to Dubai on Wednesday morning for a 10-hour layover. It wasn't too bad as I ended up hanging out in the massive airport gorging myself on Cinnabons, Burger King, and Coldstone Creamery ice cream. I savored every bite of my whopper (my last was in December), but a couple hours later my stomach started to complain about all the fat and other junk found in American food.

Another great thing about the Dubai Airport is the free wifi throughout the kilometers of indoor walkways. I was able to Skype, email, and surf the internet to help pass the time. The stores were great too, filled with many deals on quality merchandise, better than anything I have seen in Africa. Finally in the evening I caught my flight to Addis arriving just after dark to the sweet cool mountain air. My friend Jason from DRC joined me in Addis for the trip up country.

Lalibela, Ethiopia. 19 May 2011.

An early morning flight whisked us from Addis thru Gondor to Lalibela up in the mountainous north of Ethiopia. During the overcast day and through light rain showers we toured 12 ancient churches hewn out of the red rock hillsides. Centuries ago devout Christians led by Emperor Lalibela dug down into the rock to carve out multistory churches (40,000+ workers over 23 years according to our guide). Now the area is a holy land where thousands make annual pilgrimages to pray and kiss the rock walls. Tunnels and narrow pathways worn into the rock link the churches and many priests and nuns live in caves in the rock surrounding the churches.

Originally the churches had intricate paintings and carvings but now they are mostly worn away. Many of the lower rock walls and pillars are a shiny black from the faithful who kiss or the rub their foreheads against the rock. In January for the Ethiopian Christmas celebrations tens of thousands swarm the churches sleeping anywhere they can find space.

The churches are surrounded by several religious schools full of young boys sent from near and far villages to study the Holy Scriptures under the careful tutelage of their new masters. They memorize the scriptures by group repetition and the chants of the young students fill the air. Often they are sent out to beg for their support and for their instructors. They sleep huddled in groups on the floor of their master's round huts. Although many may learn to read or recite the scriptures in a couple languages, few can write after the typical four year stay in Lalibela. Afterwards some earn advanced positions in their local churches and others continue to another religious school outside of Lalibela for another seven years of study before becoming a priest.

Our guide also took us through the village and we saw the usual village family life. The women prepared millet, the kids played in the crooked muddy lanes between stone huts, and the few men to be seen around were at work as tailors, hawking trinkets, or passing by on the cobblestone road with heavy burdens on their backs. The fields outside the village were being worked by the rest of the men and were freshly plowed. It was hard to look around and not see a policeman or woman in uniform in the streets but overall the town seemed very peaceful and quiet.

Axum, Ethiopia. 20 May 2011.

A quick 30-minute early morning flight took us over the mountains from Lalibela to Axum still in Northern Ethiopia. Our guide met us at the airport and took us to our hotel on a hilltop overlooking the church to drop our bags before starting our tour. Only a dozen or so people got off the plane in Axum and it seemed like we were the only tourists at the hotel or in town.

Our first stop was the obelisks park and museum that featured the biggest one piece granite obelisks in Africa and according to our guide the largest in the world. The largest one had tumbled and broken into pieces centuries ago and two slightly shorter ones remain standing, surrounded by 60 or so smaller obelisks. A few had carved designs and windows but mostly they were smooth granite stones that served as grave markers. Underground several tombs had been excavated and the adjacent museum featured artifacts that had been recovered.

After lunch we stopped at the Queen of Sheba's pool (looks like a small reservoir but now used for religious ceremonies), explored the partially excavated palace and tombs of the Axumite Empire, and examined an ancient road marker carved in three languages on the outskirts of Axum (declaring the victories of the ruler as a warning to visitors). Near the center of Axum we also visited a large church and monastery where the guardian monks claim to protect the true Ark of the Covenant. I spoke with a monk who showed me an ancient book of illustrated scriptures and confirmed that the Arc was in the adjacent building. Outside of town, away from the Eritrean border, we toured the remnants of the Queen of Sheba's palace.

Our guide worked on several archeological digs in Axum, most recently in January 2011 with a German team that uncovered the true tomb of an Emperor of Axum. He showed us around the dig site and shared some of his research in trying to discover who was buried there. The stonework of the granite tombs was amazing with large interlocking blocks that fit together smoothly without any gaps (it's hard to find anything so well done nowadays). According to our guide, the German researchers he assisted used carbon dating on the site to place it's construction to approximately 3000 years ago.

Next to the archeological dig site we watched a group of boys play soccer on the mostly flat hilltop on the edge of town. The road from town continued past the soccer field and across the rolling hills to nearby Eritrea, just before the horizon's edge.

N'Djamena, Chad. 22 May 2011.

Jason and I arrived in N'Djamena mid-day Sunday from Ethiopia to discover that Brian, joining us from Botswana, had his luggage lost for the fifth time in ten months of traveling with South African Airways (it finally arrived six days later). Rick met us at the airport and took us to his temporary house in the expat neighborhood in the Embassy district. Normally Rick lived in Mozambique but he had been transferred to Chad following the Arab Spring uprisings to help out for a couple weeks at the U.S. Embassy and arranged our visit.

N'Djamena doesn't feel too big and most of the buildings are owned by the government and many have multi-colored uniformed Soldiers carrying guns outside. It doesn't seem like there is a set uniform for the military or police as everyone looks different, with random colors and patterns, even US military camouflage patterns.

Most of the roads are paved within city limits and the most popular mode of transportation are the moto-taxis and scooters. I haven't seen any Dala-Dalas or Car Rapides (mini-buses) and the only form of mass transportation I have seen are the old Toyota FJ-40 trucks from Cameroon marked "Goods Only" that are usually packed to the roof with baggage with another 20-30 people on top. Traffic circles are a little unusual here with people in the circle required to yield to others entering which often jams up the intersection. Solar-powered traffic lights are popping up in town and surprisingly the masses on the road obey the red lights.

I have been warned about taking pictures in Chad. It used to be illegal and now a special photography permit is required. I am not sure where to get a permit and I am sure I would still get hassled even if I had one. Sometimes its just better not to attract any attention.

Lake Chad. 23-26 May 2011.

Less than 24 hours after arriving in Chad we were heading north in a military escorted convoy heading to the Lake Chad region with an organization looking to build schools in the small neglected villages in the desert. This organization had started to build some schools in 2007 before the civil war but everything had to be abandoned as rebels swept across the country from the East. During this trip we were checking on the school construction projects that had been started and assessing the need for and survey potential locations for the construction of a couple of new schools.

About 100km outside of N'Djamena the newly paved smooth road comes to an end and the bouncing begins. The first day we drove to Elephant Rock and camped for the night in the shadow of massive stone hills, with one of course, shaped like an elephant. While one truck of soldiers drove to a nearby village to buy a goat for dinner other soldiers grabbed their AK-47s to go hunting Guinea Fowl seen on the nearby hillside. At least 20 shots later they killed one bird and started roasting it over a campfire. Meanwhile the other soldiers returned with their goat, butchered it, and threw it in a large pot over the cooking fire.

The soldiers who butchered the goat explained their tradition as they went through the process. First they laid the goat on the ground and spoke softly as they petted the goat's neck and face. A soldier explained that they were thanking the goat for its sacrifice and calming it down, eventually closing the goat's eyes before they slit the neck. As they were soothing the goat they hollowed out a section of sand beneath the neck so the blood would collect there. Once the bleeding stopped the soldiers tied a rope around the hoofs and strung the sheep from an acacia tree so the neck continued its slow drip while they skinned the goat, removing the hide in one piece. Next they quickly butchered the goat so within 20 minutes nothing was left and all the edible parts were in a large pot on an open fire. Both the goat and the fowl tasted great and in the morning we had leftover ribs and coarse salt for breakfast.

The next day we arrived in the lake region but couldn't see the lake for the trees. We tried to stay close to the lake as we drove north but kept running into thick acacia groves that scratched and tore at the Chadian soldiers sitting in the back of their open trucks. We visited three villages on the second day and found that only one of the 2007 school projects had been completed. The school was a gray concrete three-room building with two small metal shuttered windows and a metal roof. A simple blackboard had been painted on the wall and students sat on logs or bricks on the sand floors. There were no lights and no electricity.

When we drove up to the concrete school we found it empty and the local elders had to get the keys to open it. We later discovered the kids in school in a different part of the village in an open-sided straw roofed hut. The concrete school was sweltering and the small windows stopped the light breeze that made the desert heat bearable. It was no wonder that the school was still held in the same way as most of the other villages we saw, in open aired structures that blocked the sun but allowed the breeze to pass through.

Most of the teachers in Chad are community teachers that are hired by the local school village. Many of these community teachers have no formal training and are often simply the smartest guy in the village.

The further north we traveled the worse the roads became and we and our escorts had to dig out of the deep sand at least a half dozen times. The Chadians would grab branches and small bushes and jam them under the wheels to try to get tractions, but in the end we had to use metal sand ladders. We were reduced to driving 30km per hour over a torn up dirt road and eventually we called it a night after driving in the dark for two hours. The Chadians pulled over on the side of the road started a fire, butchered and feasted on another goat, and soon we were snoozing under the stars.

Day three started with more leftover roasted goat ribs for breakfast, then we checked out another village for a potential school, before driving into Bol on the north shore of Lake Chad. Bol is a district capital and has a small port, which is more of a sandy beach where pirogues (canoes) from Nigeria dock with goods for sale. I saw woven reed mats, large sacks of corn, and mango come off the small paddle and pole powered boats which were met by the local customs inspectors. It was easy to see how high the lake used to be and many of the fingers of the lake are now dry.

Twelve hours of driving later we arrived back at the end of the paved road outside of N'Djamena where the Chadian soldiers slaughtered another goat for dinner and little kids looking for food mobbed us. On the way back into town we ran out of gas but fortunately we had fuel cans in the back of the truck and were able to get on the road again, arriving well after dark, around 10pm.

N'Djamena, Chad. 27-29 May 2011.

The last couple days we have been winding things down in N'Djamena, completing reports, and preparing for upcoming trips. There isn't a whole lot to do here but wrestle with my friend's pet gazelle (this variety of gazelle is a small breed of antelope the size of a large dog) and hang out by the pool. For Memorial Day my friend had a BBQ with a roasted pig and a fish fry. We watched part of the Red Sox game and a couple expats from the community came over and had some drinks. I think we have eaten at all four of the restaurants that cater to expats and wandered around the monuments and the local market. What else is there to do in N'Djamena?

N'Djamena, Chad. 30 May 2011.

We were supposed to observe military training of the Special Anti-Terrorism Group (SATG) that was established under the U.S State Department Pan-Sahel Initiative (now Operation Enduring Freedom: Trans-Sahel) but the Commander had finally received pay for his troops and decided to hold a formation and hand out pay to his troops instead. The unit had conducted long-range patrols along the Sudanese and northern borders and occasionally found drug traffickers. Their problem was that Chad was a vast, empty country and they didn't have the resources to patrol all of it.

Limbe, Cameroon. 1 June 2011.

After a late night arrival in Yaoundé last night (took us 14 hours to fly from N'Djamena to Yaoundé on five different segments) we left early in the morning and drove to Douala. We had stopped there earlier yesterday on our aerial tour of the region but we had stupidly believed our travel agent that we couldn't get a rental car to Yaoundé so it was better to keep on flying. The drive wasn't too bad; we just had to keep dodging logging trucks carrying massive dead trees, many larger than five feet in diameter. We spent a couple hours in Douala but it wasn't too impressive for being the biggest city in Cameroon. Actually most of the time we spent in Douala was stuck in traffic.

In Douala we met the Port Authority and toured the port before heading over to the Battalion d'Intervention Rapide (BIR, also known as the Rapid Intervention Battalion). The BIR Douala facility was originally a logistics hub but had transformed into a counter-piracy command and control center. The BIR provided maritime escorts and was able to monitor the Cameroonian maritime domain and interdict unidentified vessels. Two of their recent achievements were catching pirates in March and capturing bank robbers who attempted to flee by boat.

From Douala we headed towards Mt Cameroon and the black sand beaches of Limbe. Light rain and low clouds obscured the view of the mountain and prevented us from climbing it. However, we went to the beach and I was able to rent an old plastic Bic 9-foot longboard for 5,000 CFA. Out in the warm silvery water I discovered the board was broken in two places, which made it easier to duck-dive under the wave and more comfortable to paddle (first break was near my head and the second was under my ribs). The waves were knee to thigh high and rising and I was able to catch as many waves as I wanted. I couldn't do anything aggressive with the broken board, but it was nice to get up and cruise with a couple slow turns.

Limbe nightlife is non-existent besides the few college/youth groups doing research or service projects. We ended up at a house that was converted into a restaurant at dinner time. When it came time to order we were asked if we wanted fish, chicken, or beef- the only options of the day. The fish was great and I was still totally relaxed from the first good surf session in what seemed like ages. Chad was interesting, but despite all that sand there were no waves and almost no water in Chad, even in Lake Chad.

Limbe, Cameroon. 2 June 2011.

In Limbe we toured the BIR training base and watched BIR troops in training. The total process to train a BIR soldier was ten months: three months for basic training, six months of specialized training (airborne, sniper, diver, special weapons, krav magav), followed by a month of unit specialization training as BIR units are stationed throughout the country and have different missions. We followed a patrol through a training lane, then observed squad assault, and individual marksmanship drills. At the end of the day the commander called a special formation where a soldier was disciplined for disobedience, stripped of his rank, and kicked out of the BIR. My interpreter commented that his worse crime was talking loudly while out on night missions with his unit.

Yaoundé, Cameroon. 3 June 2011.

After spending ten days in Chad I really appreciated the cool green of Cameroon. It was great to surf and hang out on the beach in Limbe and in Douala on the coast where the jungle stretched to the edge of the sea. The frequent rains and heavy clouds kept the temperatures down. On the drive back to Yaoundé we arrived back in town a couple tense hours after dark. The drive was tense because driving on the country roads in Cameroon after dark is suicidal. Vehicles just stop in the road and leave no lights on or warning markers. Motorcyclists have a crazy habit of flashing their headlight and then turning it off right as they approach you. Then there are the official and unofficial road blocks- you are lucky if you get an official one because bandits set up surprise check points and will take everything, even the car (we were warned these robberies are becoming more and more frequent).

The next morning we set out to explore Yaoundé since we had only seen it in the dark before with our late arrivals and early departures. At night the city was impressive with all the lit buildings and working street lights. In the daytime the government buildings, hotels, and other large edifices stood out even more and seemed modern for Africa.

I played a round of golf on the main course in town and the

monkeys were the primary hazard on the course. The monkeys stayed off the green but if your ball landed near the edge of the fairway the monkeys would scamper out of the woods and grab your ball and steal it or throw it in a random direction. After a while we stopped keeping track of the score due to monkey interference and played from the general area where the ball had landed.

After lunch we toured the local beer factory and discovered to the chagrin of my companions that the Yaoundé factory only did blonde beers and the Guinness was done in a neighboring town. They still enjoyed a couple local beers at the end of the tour while I choked down a variety of unusually flavored Schweppes sodas.

Back at my friend's apartment I found a smashed up Yamaha American style scooter near his parking space. He said he had brought it to Cameroon to drive around but on his very first drive in Yaoundé a car ran an intersection and smashed the scooter and threw him to the side of the road. After that he bought a used Landcruiser and watches more closely for Cameroonian drivers.

I noticed as we went out to dinner that night that there were not a lot of expats in Yaoundé and my small group of friends attracted a lot of attention. Nobody hassled us, but we stood out more than back in Dakar where there are westerners everywhere. There were also no new BMWs anywhere to be seen. I saw a couple new Mercedes E-class driven by what appeared to be government types, but besides that the perverse displays of wealth by the elites weren't evident like in many other cities (like in Dakar were you were likely to see five or more new BMW X6s every day). The people were nice and I enjoyed walking around Yaoundé.

Yaoundé, Cameroon. 5 May 2011.

Two months ago I watched Senegal narrowly defeat Cameroon in the CAF Futebol match in Dakar at the very last minute. Neither team played well in that match littered with sloppy passes and the star of the Cameroonian team, Samuel Eto'o, did absolutely nothing. As a sheer matter of coincidence we ended up in Yaoundé the same weekend as the rematch where Cameroon had to win or risk elimination from the CAF. By a miracle a friend was given five VIP tickets by Samuel Eto'o (connections through a charity expat organization) and he passed the other four onto my traveling companions and me.

Back in Dakar I had to take a taxi to about a kilometer from the stadium, walk the rest of the way, stand in line, and fight security to get in and got one of the nice concrete bench seats. In Yaoundé we got the VIP treatment with our golden tickets where we were able to drive right up to the stadium and had special reserved parking. We sat in the VIP section in nice seats and people brought us drinks and commemorative shirts. After the match the police opened a path for our vehicle and we quickly moved out of traffic back into the city (in Dakar it took us two hours to leave the stadium parking lot).

The match was one-sided with Senegal playing not to lose the entire match while Eto'o and crew took shot after shot. Fortunately for Senegal, the Lions of Terranga, the outstanding goalie never let anything in and made a series of amazing saves. The referees did their best to help the Cameroonian team, the Indomitable Lions, but Eto'o could never put the ball in the net, even once hitting the crossbar on a penalty. By the end of the match the Senegalese coach was ejected and Senegal was playing without two players and Cameroon still could not score. At the end the air went out of the crowd as the head referee blew his whistle three times to end the match. Cameroon did everything it could but Senegal somehow remained undefeated.

The crowd was depressed and walked quietly with their heads down as they left the stadium and it seemed the Senegalese were smart enough to not celebrate too loudly their victory. Later I heard that a small riot broke out near the stadium and a hotel where westerners and Senegalese visitors stayed and had to be rescued by the Police.

The next morning I caught my flight back to Senegal. I enjoyed my time in Cameroon and hope to go back some day to catch more waves, climb Mt Cameroon, and explore the rest of the country. Five days is not enough time experience Cameroon.

□

13 SOUTH AFRICA

My year in Senegal was almost over and it was time to pack up my surfboards, other few belongings, and prepare to move back to the U.S. Most of what I owned fit into a couple duffle bags and my friends had mocked me for not even having a television.

I had just enough time and money to take one final trip and visit South Africa. I had tried to visit before but it never worked out with my schedule. Brad and I had even entered the Comrades Ultra-marathon lottery and were selected to participate in the 56-mile race but Brad ended up being sick so we cancelled our participation in the race.

I had dreams of visiting and surfing South Africa ever since I learned to surf while I was in college in Hawaii. My favorite surf movie was 'Endless Summer,' filmed in the 1960s, about some surfers who travelled around the world to try and follow the surf. The first place they surfed in Africa was in Dakar, near where I surfed on a regular basis. The last place they surfed in Africa was near Durban, South Africa where they found a nearly perfect wave. I had always wanted to surf there but unfortunately I was out of time and money to include a Durban leg. Instead I focused on the more important political locations of Pretoria, Johannesburg, and Cape Town during my five-day trip to South Africa.

Pretoria, South Africa. 15 June 2011.

Driving in South Africa is crazy, especially at night in a manual transmission rental car on the wrong side of the road after a long flight from Dakar. At least I was smart enough to rent a GPS so I only took a few detours to get to my hotel in Pretoria. I had flown into Johannesburg and rented a car to drive to Pretoria since the two cities are about an hour apart and I had heard that the roads were good. It was weird to drive on a highway four or five lanes wide lit with working streetlights and without people walking on the sides of the road.

I had to keep reminding myself to stay on the left side of the road. I only had to swerve twice to get back on the left side of the road so far. Usually my loyal traveling companion, Brad from Tanzania, does all the driving in the former British colonies. Lucky for him he is on the way back to the states for vacation and I will have to visit South Africa by myself.

My flight from Dakar arrived late so I drove the entire distance between Johannesburg and Pretoria in the dark. By the time I reached the neighborhood where my hotel was located all the restaurants besides McDonalds were closed. I still didn't eat at McDonalds but I was excited to see a McDonalds with a drive thru, as there are very few on the continent outside of South Africa.

Coming from Dakar in the summer I wasn't prepared for how cold it would be in June. The southern hemisphere was already deep in winter. Despite shivering in the cold I was able to catch part of a lunar eclipse from the balcony of my hotel room. The effect of the lunar eclipse on the clear night sky made the moon look as though a brownish-purple cloud covered it.

Johannesburg, South Africa. 16 June 2011.

June 16th is Youth Day, a South African national holiday to remember the young South Africans who took to the streets in 1976 to protest new educational requirements. A new law in 1976 had required some levels of studies to be taught and completed only in Afrikaans and the teachers and students were not prepared to do it. Students organized a march to the local stadium from all the schools in the Soweto area and enroute they were met by the police who opened fire. One of the first killed was Hector Pieterson who is now honored by a museum located near where he fell. The student march and violent response by the police set off years of bloody resistance that contributed to the fall of Apartheid.

I was fortunate to be in the area for this holiday and arranged for a local tour guide to take me around to several of the significant sites. We started at the Apartheid Museum near Johannesburg where I was randomly selected to tour the museum as a Colored Non-White and entered a display that discussed the classification system that separated the population as White, Colored, and Black and attributed certain rights, privileges, and restrictions to each group. The museum then exposes the brutality of the Apartheid system with personal accounts, historical documentation, movies, newspapers, photographs, signs, etc. that were used to separate people. Whites were treated the best and had all rights and privileges, colors (usually of Asian or Indian descent), had some privileges but were still treated as a subclass, and the blacks (95% of the population) were severely restricted and had few rights. Those who protested were threatened, beaten, killed, or imprisoned.

A large part of the museum was dedicated to political prisoners and anti-Apartheid leaders with Nelson Mandela featured prominently. The films of the white police clashing with protesters, shooting and beating them were difficult to watch. It's hard to believe that all this took place during my life and even while I was in college in the US blacks in South Africa were still being violently oppressed and beaten by the Apartheid regime. What's more incredible to me is that the U.S. Government supported the Government of South Africa and considered Nelson Mandela as a terrorist (he was on our No-Fly list). No wonder why South Africans are suspicious of Americans and have a different understanding of "terrorism." It was only through terrorism or acts of terror against the government in the struggle against Apartheid that brought the former government to negotiate with the people and release political prisoners.

The next stop on my tour was the Mandela House in Soweto, which is now a swank neighborhood full of expensive BMWs and Mini Coopers. One a corner, near the top of the hill is a small red brick house where Nelson Mandela lived with his family. There isn't much to the site, but it was packed with locals and school children when I visited. Some pieces of original furniture are on display along with many photographs and quotes on the walls. It was interesting to see the site described in his autobiography, "Long Walk to Freedom."

A couple blocks away is the Hector Pieterson museum where the current President of South Africa laid a wreath earlier in the day at the dedication of a new monument to celebrate Youth Day. Again the museum was packed with hundreds of school children learning about the student uprising and adults wearing their old school ties or colors and remembering. The stories of people who were a part of the march are posted on the walls along with photographs of the march and ensuing violence at the hands of the police. This wasn't something in the distant past for the people walking through the museum, but still recent events that most of the population had lived through. I wonder how long it will take for these wounds to heal.

At the end of the long day visiting museums and touring the city we stopped at a roadside Braai (barbeque) on the way to Pretoria and grilled our dinner. At the Braai you select your meat then throw it on the outside grill with 20 or so other people sharing strands of wire to flip the meat. Once the meat was done my black tour-guide and I sat down at the nearby picnic table and discussed the day, his experiences during the protests, and what it all meant. We also talked about my other travels in Africa and my tour-guide was surprised to learn that the rest of the continent was different. He had never left his country and only compared himself to the US, Europe, or Australia as those were the only places he had seen on TV. He thought his country was bad with corruption and unemployment but was amazed when I mentioned Chad or the electricity problems in Senegal.

Pretoria, South Africa. 17 June 2011.

Today I visited the U.S. Mission to South Africa where officers described South Africa as a mix of first and third world economies with over 600 U.S. companies present in South Africa and the U.S. was the second largest importer of South African goods. On the political side the Nelson Mandela's ANC was still dominant political party and they still remembered U.S. support of the apartheid government.

While South Africa had contributed peacekeeping troops to DRC and South Sudan they were reluctant to participate in AMISOM. South Africa was also a member of the State Partnership program and teamed up with the state of New York and participated in some AFRICOM supported exercises. South Africa has an extensive navy and air force and is the producer of the MRAP armored personnel carriers used by the U.S. in Iraq and Afghanistan. It's military industrial complex exports internationally and takes care of most of its own military needs.

One of the biggest U.S. government programs in South Africa is the PEPFAR program with over $600 million per year in funding and activities.

I spent much of the afternoon wandering around Pretoria, amazed at how green and clean it was. The government buildings and embassies were nice, and I saw the most white people that I had seen so far in South Africa at the Bulls Rugby Stadium where I ate lunch. The restaurant looks over the practice pitch where we saw several players jogging around. Everybody was excited because the following day was the traditional rivalry/grudge match against the Sharks. Tickets sold out weeks ago and everyone I talked to said it should be a good match, but of course the Bulls would be victorious. Fortunately the night before the movie 'Invictus' about the South African rugby team was on TV so I was up on my rugby. I "get" rugby and have a lot of respect for the players but Cricket is still a total mystery to me.

Cape Town, South Africa. 18 June 2011.

I took the 8am flight from Johannesburg and two hours later arrived in Cape Town on the coast. The shuttle to take me to the hotel didn't show up so I hired a cab driver to take me to the V&A waterfront where I would be staying. It turned out the driver was also a tour guide and he offered to take me around for the day. In the end the full day private guided tour cost me R1200 ($175 USD), way less than what the hotels and tour agencies prices.

My priority for this trip was to see Robben Island, but the ferry to the Island was completely sold out and there was a line of people standing by to see if they could steal any of the "no show" slots. Turns out that none of the standby passengers made it to the island that day.

It was a beautiful day, the sun was shining, and the sky was blue with a light cool breeze. I had to wear a jacket as we headed up to the top of Table Mountain by cable car. The car ride both ways cost R180 ($26 USD) but some choose the two hour hike to the top instead or rappel (abseiling) and hike down. The cable car was cool because it completed one full rotation on the descent or ascent to the top, giving all passengers a great view of the mountain and cape. On top the winds were stronger and it was a little cooler but the views were amazing. There is also an extensive trail system on natural granite paths lined by small bushes and reeds that extend to both ends of the plateau and down to the ocean below. On the way down we saw a group of climbers scaling a multi-pitch route up the granite cliffs.

My next stop was Cape Point, the southern tip of the African continent and along the route we stopped at several scenic overlooks and small white towns. We did stop in one black township and drove around. Most of the shacks were nicer than the villages in the rest of the parts of Africa I have visited as they had solid walls, roof, doors, a paved floor, electricity, and water. People weren't cooking in the street over charcoal stoves and I didn't see any public bathrooms. Most of the areas were pretty clean. In the Cape Town region is seemed that the shantytowns were nicer than even in Johannesburg where the "Mandela Towns" were crammed together in fields outside of the city.

We also stopped at an Ostrich Farm on the way to Cape Point and a national park but didn't see many animals besides ostriches despite the many road signs to watch for Orangutans or Urdu. The parking lot at Cape Point was jammed with buses and tourists climbed over rocks and fought for pictures behind a sign in English and Afrikaans that declared this to be the end of the world (or southern point of the continent). The water was a cool blue color but shifted violently and the oceans collided with currents pushing against each other. There were some good size waves but nothing was surfable. I was surprised to find that the water was warm and happy to see that it was clean and free of the garbage that litters so many African beaches.

On the way back I stopped in a small town and visited a Penguin colony where several young chicks were molting. The flightless birds just waddled around or sat and were patient with the 30 or so tourists that swarmed around them and zoomed their telephoto lenses into their dens. There was no separation between the people and the penguins and it was cool to have them all around me.

Our next stop was a small fishing town where we got fish and chips on the wharf at a local bar frequented by people of all backgrounds. The food was outstanding and the people were outgoing with the waitress telling me she saw me on the "Ricki Lake" show. Coloreds and whites freely shared their apartheid experiences growing up in the area. They laughed together as they told some funny stories and repeated several times that as kids they played together and they thought Apartheid was a weird exterior thing forced on them by the state and enforced by police but didn't really affect the spirit or way of life of the locals.

Just before going over the hill back to the hotel we stopped at a shark lookout above an awesome surf break that had long lines of chest-high waves. Shark Watchers manned the post looking for dark shadows under the water with polarized binoculars. If they saw a shark they would radio down to the lifeguards on the beach below and they would close the beach until the shark moved on. The lady on duty said the last shark spotting was in March but in the past many surfers had been eaten there.

The day's tour of the Cape Town area was very interesting, especially since my guide was a white Afrikaner who had an opposite experience with Apartheid and the following unity government than my guide in Johannesburg the day before. Both guides had legitimate experiences but lived very different lives. From what I saw it seems that the black South Africans lives had improved significantly but he was still not as fortunate nor had the same opportunities as the white South African.

Cape Town, South Africa. 19 June 2011.

When I woke up it was pouring rain outside. My guide yesterday said we had been fortunate with the great weather yesterday as the day before it had rained all day and Sunday was expected to rain again. I checked out of my hotel early and caught a cab across town to church in Mowbray but got stuck there. Perhaps because it was Father's Day or just a Sunday morning there were no taxis to be seen anywhere. So after a quick egg McMuffin at McDonalds (tasted great! My only McDonalds experience in Africa) I started walking back to Cape Town.

I walked for two hours though all kinds of neighborhoods and shopping areas in a light drizzle. Nobody messed with me and it was kind of like walking through worn out or depressed downtown areas in small town America. I passed a couple mega-Churches where singing and preaching could be heard from blocks away but it seemed like nobody cared that I was walking through.

Eventually I made it to downtown Cape Town and the European-styled palace with large monuments out front, facing a large square. The square was surrounded by a large bus station, huge shopping malls, and skyscrapers. This part of town reminded me of a European city with detailed monuments, nice sidewalks, and tall buildings with glass walls.

The wet city streets were abandoned and even the mall was closed, so I was surprised when I arrived at the V&A (Victoria and Alfred) Waterfront to bustling crowds. The shopping center at V&A was packed with thousands of locals and tourists who were mostly white. There were tons of great bars and restaurants at the waterfront and boats offering tours of the port and area, including to Robben Island. However, the ferry to Robben Island was closed for the day due to high seas and the people who had tickets were out of luck.

I ended up eating lunch at a local restaurant and checking out the shops and displays at the waterfront before heading to the airport later that afternoon. From Cape Town I flew through Johannesburg back to Dakar arriving at 6am the next morning.

Five days is not enough time to see South Africa, and I didn't get a chance to surf with my busy schedule and bad weather. I would also like to return and watch the Great White Sharks hunting seals where they attack from below, launching the seals into the air and catching them in their jaws. I will have to come back later.

14 LEAVING DAKAR

Dakar, Senegal. 20 June 2011.

While I was in South Africa Jake and Jason from DRC had come to visit and borrowed my Landcruiser to drive around and had driven out to Kedagou (where they blew a tire on the bush trails near the border with Guinea), Touba, and down to Banjul in the Gambia. When I got back we tried to find a replacement tire for the truck since the tire was ruined with a sidewall blowout, but it turns out that my Landcruiser was a custom special ordered model.

The 17-inch rims are unusual for Senegal and even the Toyota dealer did not have them in stock and couldn't order replacement tires. At his suggestion we tried to throw some 16inch wheels on the truck but the rims wouldn't fit the oversized brake calipers. Finally we were able to to find a used replacement tire through a friend of a worker at a tire dealer who had a small shop next to the Grand Mosque for 40,000 CFA (we were able to negotiate the price down from 75,000 CFA). The tire had a couple plugs in it but the patches looked good, so at least I can use this as a spare until I can figure out how to get a replacement tire from the states.

The moral of the story is if you are going to bring a truck to Africa make sure you can not only get spare parts and have mechanics that know how to work on try truck, but that common things like tires are available. If not, bring the tires with you.

Saint Louis, Senegal. 24-25 June 2011.

Yesterday morning my friends, who were visiting from the States, and I departed Dakar just before the riots started. We had planned to visit Lompoul and Saint Louis and had reservations at the tent camp out in the small patch of desert by the sea in Lompoul. The day before riot police had taken up positions around key government buildings and when we left at 7am the National Assembly had been barricaded and riot police were in position at key intersections throughout the city, even into Rufisque. Things were still calm and it seemed like it would be a normal day but before we arrived in Thies I got a phone call from a friend warning me to stay out of the downtown area as over 10,000 protesters had blocked off the area and were throwing rocks at cars and burning tires. As an American living in Senegal I subscribed to the U.S. Embassy Warden Systems so I received emails about demonstrations and I started getting text messages detailed the progress of the protesters as they moved about town.

In Thies we arrived in town as several hundred protesters reached the large traffic circle at the center of town. They seemed to be marching peacefully and were escorted by police. Other police with riot shields and gear stood at the corners but nobody was fighting. At lunch our waiter became upset when I commented on how peaceful the march was and he wanted me to know that he was angry too and everybody needed to know that things had to change.

After leaving Thies we headed north to Kebemer and turned left at the horse statue and drove out to Lompoul village. There we met our guide who led us into a patch of orange desert surrounded by eucalyptus trees where we rode camels and slept in tents among the sandy dunes. Unfortunately there were no bed nets in the tents again and we were harassed by mosquitos throughout the night.

The next morning after a light breakfast we powered our way out of the sand dunes back to the road and drove down to Lompul by the sea and checked out the fish drying stations. Then we turned around and drove the rest of the way to Saint Louis and checked into our hotel. That afternoon we hired a horse buggy and guide who drove us around the island and fishing village on the Langue de Barberie. All the local kids were out swimming in the green river and catching small fish by hand lines. We didn't see many tourists around and the vendors were more aggressive than normal and prices for the trinkets seemed higher than usual. My American friends enjoyed walking around but by the end of the day we were all burned out by the kids who constantly thronged us with their hands out demanding a "cadeau" (gift) or "argent" (money).

Saturday morning when we loaded our bags into the Landcruiser a mob of kids was waiting for us and banged on the windows of the restaurant while we ate breakfast. On the way off the island we stopped at the Aeropostal Museum and for 1,500 CFA each we got to read old poster boards about how airmail traffic used to be routed from South America across the Atlantic to Saint Louis, then north over the desert to France. The highlight of the museum was a couple old model airplanes under hazy plastic domes.

The ride back to Dakar was pretty easy and the weather was cooler due to some rain that fell during the night. Many of the streets in Thies were flooded and the car washers were disappointed that they couldn't wash cars in the light sprinkles that fell in the afternoon. We did make another stop on the way home just north of Thies to buy some hand-woven baskets. I highly recommend checking out the roadside basket and pottery vendors just north of Thies on the road to Saint Louis. The prices for the baskets were 80% lower than in Dakar and the people were very glad to see us. My friends and I each spent about 20,000 CFA ($40 USD) and loaded up the back of the Landcruiser with all sizes and colors of baskets.

Back in Dakar things seemed almost normal with a few more police in riot gear fewer hanging out in the Place d'Independence, in front of the Presidential Palace, and the Ministry of Interior. The only real damage I could see in my quick drive through the area was that the head-high green metal fence between the Cathedral and the Catholic School was bent down flat to the ground. The only windows smashed just happened to be the ones at the entry to my apartment. The guard told me that a mob had come down the street and gathered in front of the building and was throwing stones and trying to get in the building, but eventually were driven away or moved on to another area. I guess I should be glad I was out of town.

Dakar, Senegal. 26 June 2011.

Heavy overhead waves on the west coast of Dakar today. My friend "Happy" took Jason and me from DRC out to Club Med for some great surf. Club Med is usually a meter higher than the other breaks on the left side and accessed by a long paddle or 300-meter stumble along slick rocks on the edge of the water.

We ended up surfing a couple breaks near the westernmost point in Africa while Happy's girlfriend took a photographs of us from the rocks. Happy is a good surfer and works at a local surf camp but is willing to take people around the area to find good surf breaks. He said he can guarantee he can get you barreled (I'm still working on that). There were a few solid French expats in the water too that were getting incredible rides on long rights. You just had to watch out for the partially submerged cannon located where the wave was breaking.

Unfortunately I got caught inside by an overhead set and slammed on the rocks and had to bail when I saw my right foot was bleeding heavily. Thankfully I didn't see any urchins.

The next day Jason went back to Kinshasa and the movers came to my apartment and packed up all my surfboards and gear to ship back to the United States. As it took a couple days for the gash on my foot to heal that last surf trip was my final paddle out in Africa before I caught my flight to New England to begin my studies at Boston University on a Masters of International Relations with a certificate in African Studies. With any luck I'll be surfing the cold New England breaks within a couple weeks and back in Africa as soon as I graduate. Hopefully, somewhere else where the water is warm, the people are nice, and the waves are head-high and glassy.

EPILOGUE

Kampala, Uganda. May-June 2012.

After completing my first year at Boston University in the Masters of International Relations graduate program and participating in the African Studies program, my buddy Brad invited me to come out to Uganda to conduct research for my thesis on counterinsurgency (COIN) related to the Lord's Resistance Army (LRA). Brad had been transferred from the U.S. Embassy in Tanzania to the U.S. Embassy in Uganda and knew a couple people I could interview for my thesis. In May 2012 I once again departed for Africa for a thirty-day research trip.

In preparation for the trip I read a number of published books and articles on Joseph Kony and the LRA, kept abreast of LRA activity via websites like the LRA tracker, which reported the location and interaction of the latest LRA attacks in central Africa, and interviewed a couple American military officers on COIN theory. The Kony 2012 campaign was at its strongest and even Boston University had posters and flyers all over campus advocating greater US involvement in the hunt for the LRA leaders. The most interesting current military action was the deployment of 100 US Special Forces troops to central Africa to serve as advisors and provide technical assistance to Ugandan and other troops in the region in the counter-LRA fight.

I had prepared a list of survey questions to ask Ugandan military personnel (enlisted and officers), as well as political leaders and villagers. Unfortunately a few days after I arrived in Kampala an American researcher was arrested by the Ugandan government for conducting an unsanctioned survey. This put a damper on conducting personal research as I wasn't able to secure permission from the Ugandan government to conduct my survey and I did not want to end up in an Ugandan prison. Instead I informally asked questions of the people I met, visited war memorials and official sites, and bought as many books as possible by Ugandan authors on the subject.

One of the sites I was able to visit was a war memorial in a small village in the Luwero triangle, the former base of President Museveni's National Resistance Movement (NRM). As an American military officer interested in Ugandan military history I was introduced to the village Chief and the District President who arranged for a visit to the shrine and a tour of the area. He also tasked a local reporter to tag along and take photos and publish a story on my visit. The simple shrine was located on a hill outside of the village that overlooked a vast dense forest and was the internment site of the remains of many NRM war heroes.

Uganda is a major troop contributing country to the African Union mission to Somalia (AMISOM) and the U.S. has trained over 50 battalions for the fight against Islamic militant extremists in Somalia. The bulk of these AMISOM forces are trained at a training site several hours outside of Kampala. The base can accommodate battalions of over 500 troops at a time and features convoy live fire training with armored vehicles with a v-shaped hull (to deflect improvised explosive device blasts), and a village to replicate combat in urban terrain.

I was able to visit during a convoy live fire lane where a column of twelve vehicles sped down a dirt road until they were ambushed. The Ugandan troops dismounted their vehicles and engaged pop-up targets and assaulted the targets before remounting their vehicles and continuing down the road. On another lane we watched Ugandan troops hike through the forest to attack a terrorist camp. The troops established their support by fire machine gun position that provided cover for the rest of the troops while they climbed up through the brush to the edge of the camp. Upon the pre coordinated signal (whistle blasts and a white star cluster) the machine gun position stopped firing and the troops swarmed through the village shooting pop-up targets and capturing terrorist equipment.

As with any trip with Brad in Africa we had to schedule some fun activities. We visited the source of the White Nile River in Jinja, near the border with Kenya. We also rafted the rapids on the Nile River with a local guide company. Many expats warned us not to get in the

Nile River due the threat of schistosomiasis, a parasite endemic in slow moving freshwater in Africa but we didn't have any problems. The risk of schistosomiasis was throughout and Brad had managed to contract it earlier in Dar es Salaam when their household water tank was infected. The rapids were huge Class V sections that would swallow up the entire raft and often throwing paddlers into the churning white water. Fortunately there was a flotilla of very skilled Ugandan kayakers that escorted us down the river and would collect the swimmers after the rapids and bring us back to the raft. In the calmer parts of the river we could see mosquito traps that researchers used to study West Nile Virus as it originated from the region. Luckily, none of us contracted any illnesses.

While I was in Kampala, Brad's driver died in a late night motorcycle accident and as the employer Brad was invited to participate in the funeral in a small village near Fort Portal on the Western border of Uganda. Brad invited me to come along for the funeral and we traveled for several hours to the mountainous border near the Democratic Republic of the Congo. The region is famous for its snow-capped mountains in the Rwenzori Mountains of the Moons national park.

The funeral was interesting as we were first invited to view the body and then seated in the front as special guests. Then the local pastor gave an hour-long speech in a local language we didn't understand, followed by the brother, and then Brad. After Brad's speech a choir sang and the body was interred in a freshly dug grave near the house in a field of maize. A large banquet with local foods like matoke, plantains, and some kind of meats was served to all the guests and the entire village turned out to eat.

The funeral and feast were all paid by the employer, exhausting the death gratuity and leaving the spouse and two daughters without any money. The day after the driver died, his brother made the long drive from Fort Portal to claim anything of value in the house as by their tradition the spouse and daughters did not have any claim to his possessions as there was no male heir. Fortunately, the grieving spouse was able to move the television, fridge, and the deed to the house to an acquaintance's house on the other side of town so the family members weren't able to acquire them. After the funeral was complete, Brad provided some additional funds and set up a scholarship fund for the daughters to pay their school fees.

Unfortunately traffic accidents kill dozens every day in Kampala and I was even hit by a motorcycle one morning when I was out for a run with Brad. We were running along the side of the road in a residential community and motorcycles were swerving among cars and pedestrians and one clipped my arm, almost knocking me down. If the motorcyclist had managed to hook my arm with his mirror he could have dragged me down the road or more severely injured me. Breaking bones in Uganda can be a serious emergency due to the level of medical care available and I most likely would have needed to have been flown out of Uganda for medical care.

While in Uganda I was notified that my first long term assignment in Africa would be at the U.S. Embassy in N'Djamena, Chad as soon as I completed my master's degree at Boston University. I would defend my thesis in December 2012, graduate in January 2013, and report the next month to the desert oasis on the Chari River.

US ARMY FOREIGN AREA OFFICER PROGRAM

Foreign Area Officers (FAOs) are military officers who are regionally focused experts working in U.S. Embassies around the world. FAOs focus on political-military activities and possess "a unique combination of strategic focus, regional expertise, with political, cultural, sociological, economic, and geographical awareness, and a foreign language proficiency in at least one of the dominant languages in their specified region." FAOs serve as the Defense Attaché or the Security Assistance Officer while assigned to an embassy but may also serve as country desk officers, planners, or liaison officers at the geographic combatant command (such as U.S. Africa Command) or in the Pentagon.

In these roles a FAO is expected to be an expert on all issues related to their region of expertise. In the embassy the FAO is the senior military advisor to the Ambassador and on staff the FAO advises his leadership, providing cultural expertise and situational awareness. Over the course of their career and varied experiences the FAO develops and maintains enduring relationships with foreign leaders and provides nuanced advice.

U.S. Army FAOs are selected in their seventh year of service after they have proved themselves as company commanders and demonstrated diplomatic skills, maturity, and fiscal responsibility. The three phases of the Army training program are language training, in region training, and a graduate-level education. The total training time to train an Army FAO is approximately three years with a year scheduled for each phase.

Language training is conducted at the Defense Language Institute in Monterey, California. The course length depends on the languages studied. Native speakers with advanced degrees in the target language instruct 40-hours per week in a classroom setting administering reading, listening, and speaking language tests. In my case as I already spoke Portuguese I studied French at the Defense Language Institute and earned an Associate's Degree in French.

In Region Training is a one-year assignment in the geographic region in order to gain expertise through visiting sites, meeting with officials, practicing foreign language skills, and experiencing the local culture. The FAO develops a detailed program of instruction, which specifies learning objectives related to U.S. policy development, U.S. military involvement with regional militaries, security assistance activities, and embassy administration. For my program of instruction I focused on regional stability and used my trips as opportunities to interview U.S. and local officials as well as non-governmental organizations and regular people on the streets. Due to the sensitive nature of these discussions I was not able to detail the greater part of my activities in Africa in this book.

A modest budget is provided for travels within the region for official activities and all expense vouchers are scrutinized and audited to avoid abuse of funds. I also combined my travel with my colleagues in order to reduce expenses and often ended up sleeping on the floor to keep lodging expenses down! I paid for the fun trips to see the gorillas, surfing, and other activities out of my own personal funds.

Graduate school is the final phase of the training of a FAO, where the individual attends an approved graduate school to earn a master's degree in international relations or a similar degree with a focus on their region of expertise. Most FAOs participate in a 12-month compressed program and I was fortunate to attend Boston University where I earned a Master's degree in International Relations and a certificate in African Studies. My travels in Africa during in region training were a great preparation for graduate school and I was able to enhance my understanding of what I experienced first-hand and the complex interactions in play among governments, clans, and non-governmental organizations locally, bilaterally and regionally.

☐

ABOUT THE AUTHOR

Arnie Hammari is a U.S. Army Foreign Area Officer specializing in Sub-Saharan Africa who has worked at various U.S. Embassies in Africa and with Combined Joint Task Force- Horn of Africa in Djibouti. A career military officer, Arnie has served across the United States, Europe, Afghanistan, and Africa. He is currently stationed in Germany with U.S. Africa Command Headquarters.

www.ingramcontent.com/pod-product-compliance
Lightning Source LLC
Chambersburg PA
CBHW050448290526
45786CB00006B/2203